GW01607247

‘Epic’ Voyage, Tamar to Truro

David Weston

'Epic' Voyage
Tamar to Truro

David Weston Gallery
Mevagissey Cornwall England

Published in October 1992 by
David Weston Gallery
Mevagissey, Cornwall PL26 6UB
England

Reprinted 1993

ISBN 0 9517290 1 2

Printed by Blackfords of Cornwall
Holmbush, St. Austell PL25 3JL

Contents

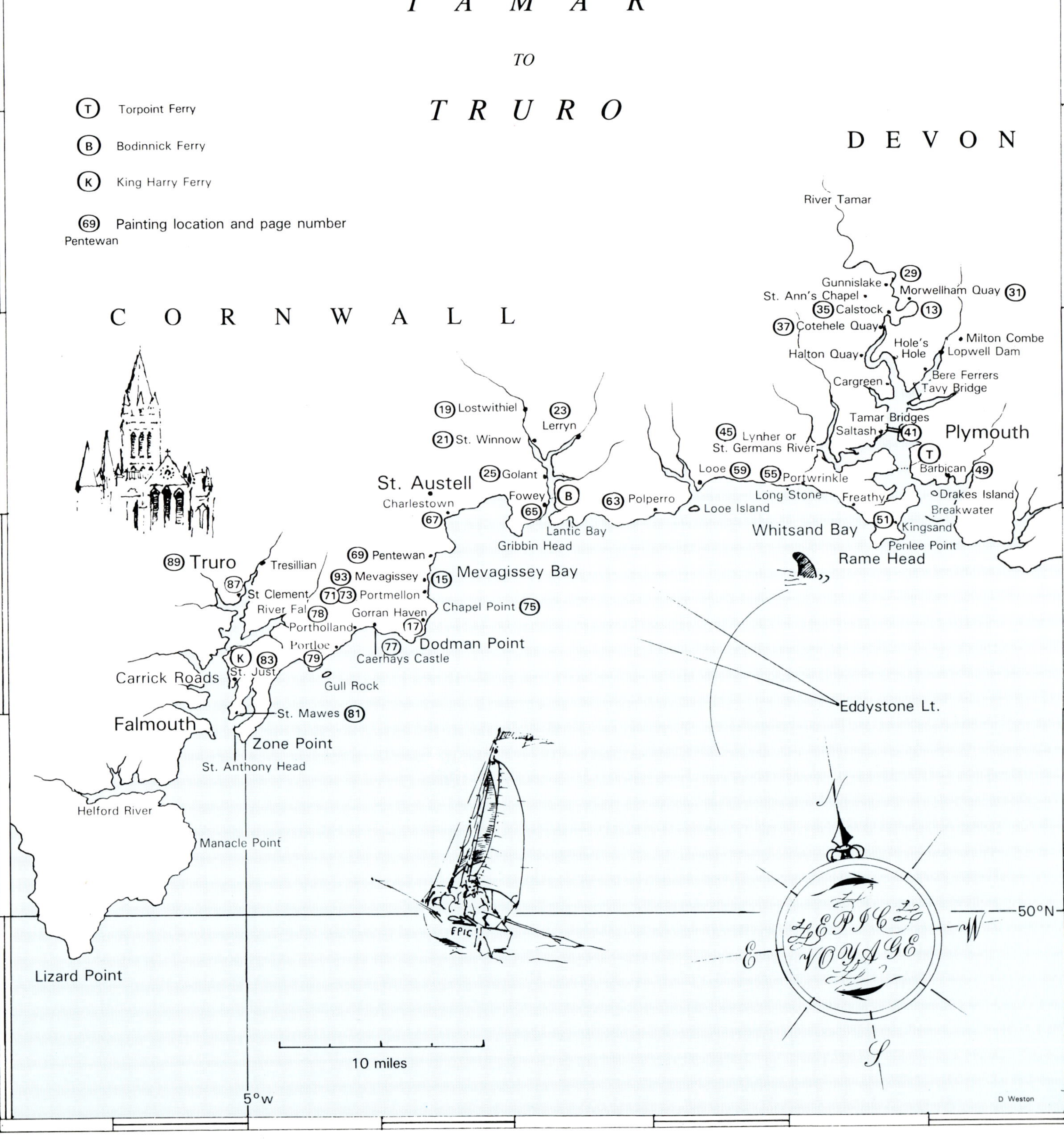
TAMAR
TO
TRURO
Torpoint Ferry
Bodinnick Ferry
King Harry Ferry
Painting location and page number
Pentewan
DEVON
CORNWALL
River Tamar
Gunnislake
St. Ann's Chapel
Morwellham Quay
Calstock
Cotehele Quay
Milton Combe
Hole's Hole
Lopwell Dam
Halton Quay
Bere Ferrers
Cargreen
Tavy Bridge
Tamar Bridges
Saltash
Plymouth
Lostwithiel
Lerryn
St. Winnow
Lynher or St. Germans River
Barbican
Golant
Looe
Portwrinkle
St. Austell
Fowey
Long Stone
Freathy
Drakes Island
Charlestown
Polperro
Looe Island
Breakwater
Lantic Bay
Whitsand Bay
Kingsand
Gribbin Head
Penlee Point
Pentewan
Rame Head
Truro
Tresillian
Mevagissey
Mevagissey Bay
St Clement
Portmellon
River Fal
Gorran Haven
Chapel Point
Portholland
Portloe
Dodman Point
St. Just
Caerhays Castle
Carrick Roads
Gull Rock
Eddystone Lt.
St. Mawes
Falmouth
Zone Point
St. Anthony Head
Helford River
Manacle Point
N
E
W
S
EPIC VOYAGE
50°N
Lizard Point
10 miles
5°W
D Weston

Illustrations

'Epic' Voyage, Tamar to Truro

Preamble

The oceans had backed the river fifteen miles up the valley to where I stood beside Epic. Soon the moon would release the waters and my elemental journey would begin. Tide and wind (with a dash of rowing) would propel me and partly dictate the course. To explore at leisure and record through watercolour the upper reaches of creeks, quiet backwaters and rugged coastline was the aim. I would travel without the help of an engine—unnoticed rather than unwelcome.

I should have known better—I had reason to know better!

My voyaging was most unpredictable.

'Somewhat tired I floated in a metaphysical as well as a nautical sense and the feeling of unreality gave free reign to the wandering of my 'other mind'. Around 3:30, from my exceptionally low vantage point, *'I gazed at a frogman's masked head! It was two or three yards away and only vaguely discernible in the gloom. The helmet moved slowly towards Epic. I kept very still.'* '

What led to that strange episode?

An introduction is called for:-

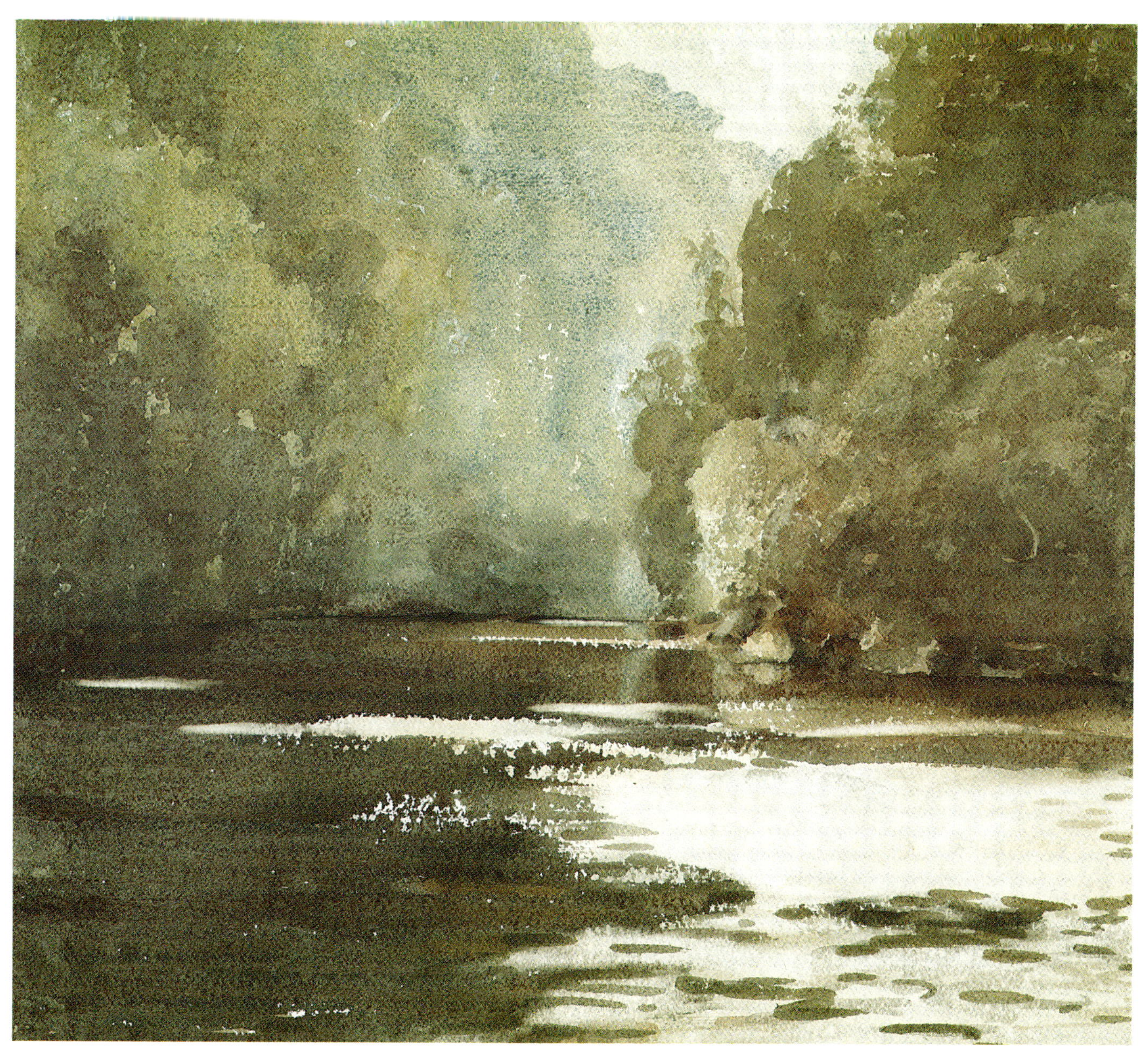

TRANQUIL TAMAR

Introduction

A year previously, when selling the resulting publication of a painting trip to North West Turkey, I was asked to produce something similar with a theme closer to home. (I live in the fishing village of Mevagissey, mid-way along the south Cornwall coast). But what angle? I had sailed a little so, why not a sailing/painting trip. The tidal rivers in the locality appealed and apart from a few stretches I had not explored them. The river Tamar, dividing Devon and Cornwall, would be a good place to start; so that summer I planned to journey no further afield than my own backyard.

On a sunny day in early May I drove to Weirhead at Gunnislake – where the tidal section of the Tamar begins. The weir pool was protected by a large locked wire-meshed gate, and not wishing to set a definite time or date for the start of my trip I sought a more accessible (and less intimidating) launching site. Just two miles down river lies Morwellham Quay – a thousand year old copper port, reclaimed from nature's advances and open to the public. I visited the historic site where a member of staff in period costume ushered me into the Ship Inn Restaurant. I was joined by the Director – his garb reminded me of Isambard Kingdom Brunell whose famous bridge I was soon to know more intimately. Gary (when not wearing a top hat) is a watercolourist – a painter of the Tamar Valley. I would launch at Morwellham.

As I hoped to complete the trip in about two, two week sessions around June when the hours of darkness were least, I needed to acquire and equip a vessel without delay. A light traditional gaff-rigged, tan sailed, ten foot clinker dinghy would have suited me. In mid May I saw, lying on the mud in Mevagissey Inner Harbour, a ten foot traditional clinker dinghy which was used as a punt (a fishing boat tender). It had once sailed and sported a centre-board case, rowlock points and fittings for mast and rudder. The following day in the Harbour Office, Jim – the Master, told me that the punt, which we could see moored in the outer harbour, was awaiting the owner's return from fishing. Later, to my request for temporary punt captaincy, Michael replied in the affirmative.

"... and there are no leaks, I've glassed over the hull centre-board aperture!"

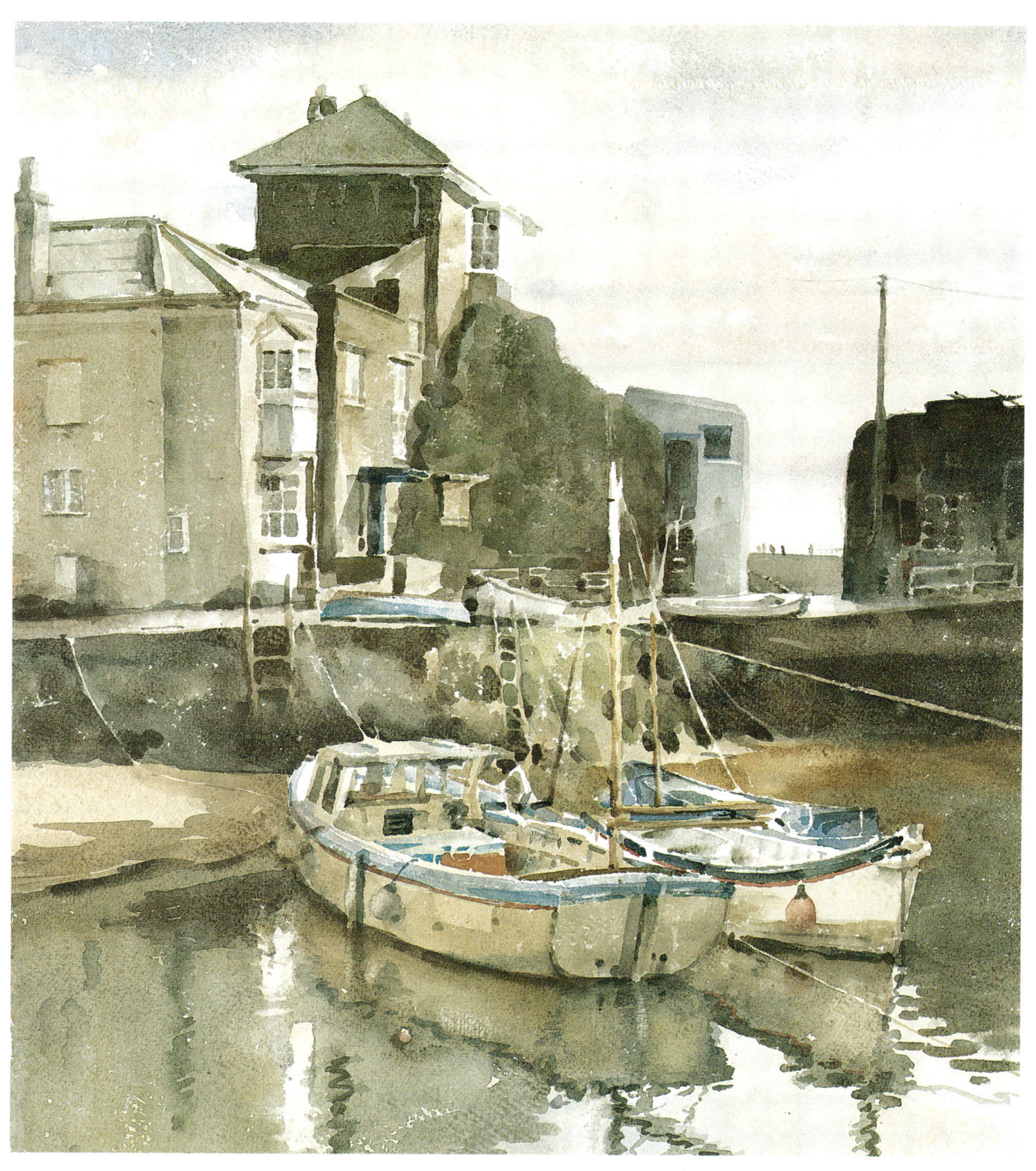

THE WATCH HOUSE, Mevagissey

My search continued. A possible boat at Gorran Haven—a perfect little gem in the harbourside boathouse, but it could not be spared. Harbourmaster Dick, thought J. Fuge, Boatbuilder at Golant on the Fowey River, might be able to help. The renovation of a slender, half deck keelboat was nearing completion in the shed—the beautiful lines of the old boat gave me pleasure, but assistant boatbuilder Luck gave me none regarding my quest.

I ceased indirect boat hunting and paid a visit to The Boat Market at Lostwithiel—at the head of the Fowey River. Amid shiny plastic craft of all sizes lay an aged Mirror dinghy. The ravages of time and the well patched hull were mostly hidden beneath a new coat of sky blue paint. The eleven foot Mirror was basically sound, being well built to a robust design. It has two blunt ends and the front one was a bit rotten, but fortunately the defect was well above the waterline. Included in the price were the spars, rigging, sails, centre-board and rudder—it was ready to sail. Inside the hull were several gallons of 'occasional showers', proving the boat was fairly watertight. The drain hole is in the stern and the little dinghy had been tipped forward, half off its trolley—so was I. A deposit was placed on the first boat looked at with intent to buy. A traditional craft with classic character had eluded me, but I was happy with my snap decision. It was not the most beautiful craft in the world, and common in the numerical sense also—which meant it had been well proven. Launching and retrieving solo would be quite easy, and the comparatively flat bottom meant it would float in three or four inches of water, and hopefully not become a stick in the mud.

I think it had rained every day in June up to the 14th, so I was not surprised to be fitting rowlock mountings at the Boatmarket in the pouring rain. Three days later and a quarter of a mile away, between showers, I painted the bridge and pool from where I would begin my shakedown journey to Fowey.

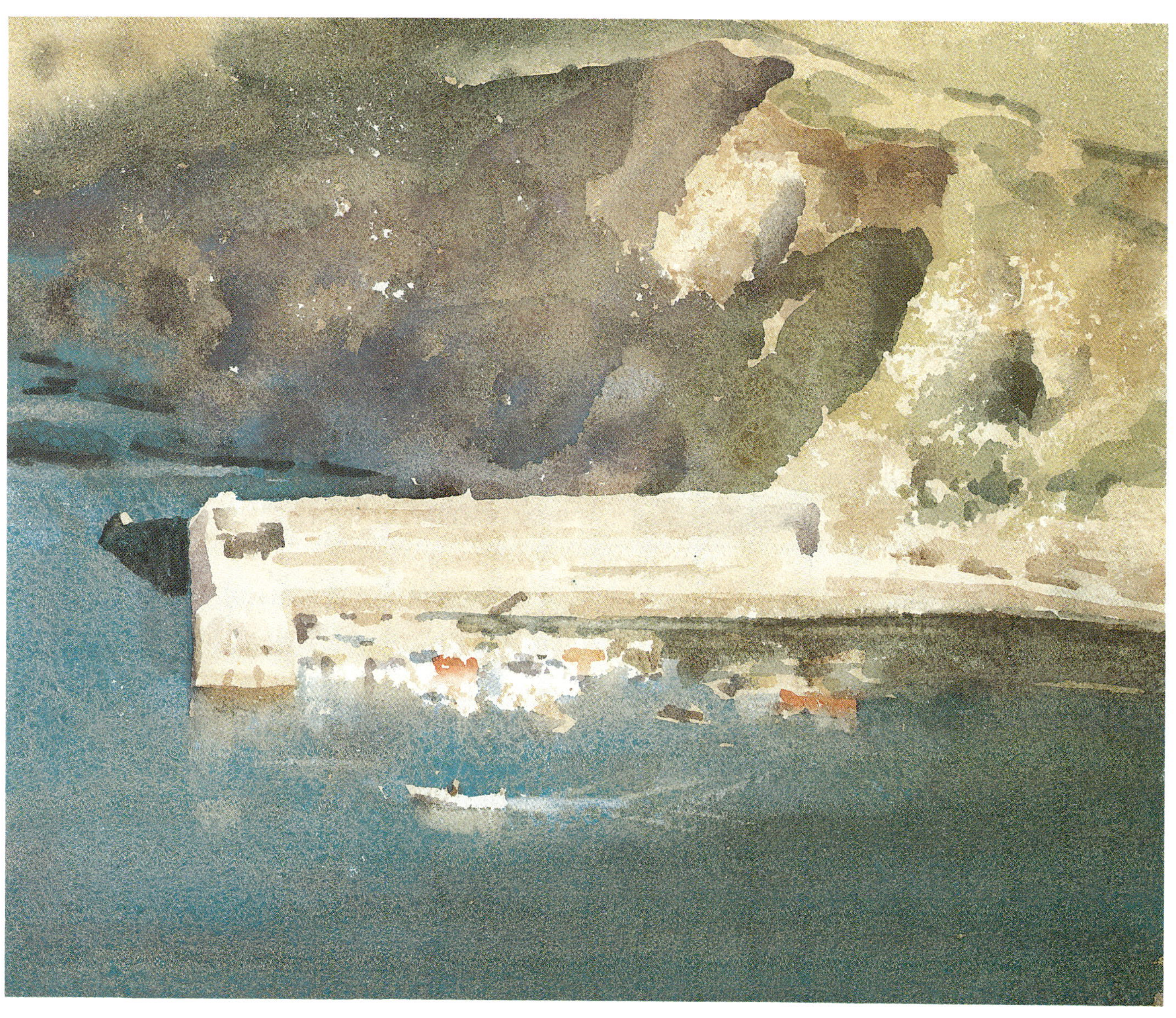

GORRAN HAVEN

Occasional token waves were flipping and swishing up to Epic's sun-warmed stern as I wandered up the steep, narrow hill between tightly packed old stone cottages.

Shakedown

Setting out in sunshine dreaming,
no thought of nature's dark side scheming.

Thursday 20th dawned fair, preceding a hot summer's day. At 12:30 I trundled the trolley with Mirror, over a level crossing, across the old river bridge and down to the water's edge. The bridge pool was full and still, and covered the shingle from where I painted a few days before. On the grassy bank in hot sunshine, Julia my wife helped me raise the mast then dump half a car full of gear into the dinghy. By 1:15 the river level began to drop. I pushed the boat into the water and stepped in between the jumble, quickly sitting down to gain stability. I was afloat for the first time in the nameless boat.

I rowed clumsily round the pool for a minute or so, and with the gravel making contact with the hull, drifted downstream waving to Julia and guiding the mast-head through the trees. Gently rowing I slipped away from Lostwithiel. I passed several craft up to twenty feet in length which were on moorings or tied to the bank—they grounded for all but a few hours a day. The river gradually widened as the backs of buildings gave way to grassy meadows. The flow downstream was still very sedate*, and I lay on my back on the pile of gear and watched the mast turn lazy circles against a few cottonwool clouds. The tidal free ride I utilized as one might a bus service. Though the timetable was reliable, times were not always convenient, but as they were a little later each day I had no excuse if I missed it. I had been underway half an hour when a young couple walking by the river turned back to Lostwithiel—I saw no one else till after nightfall.

A mile or so downstream I tied up to a little timber jetty set at right-angles to the wooded left bank. The river had increased to a good walking pace and the boat swung to a taut rope, the water chuckling round her. Two small boats were on the bank above the high water line near a bench from which one should have been able to enjoy the idyllic setting. Unfortunately, swarming bees from a nest in a nearby tree-trunk hastened my departure and I continued my leisurely drift while setting about a sun-warmed Mars bar—the melted chocolate had stuck to the wrapper, providing mè with several minutes enjoyable licking. I thought of Winnie The Pooh—must have been the bees.

*From high tide, the speed of the current increases for about three hours, then decreases for the same period to low water. The rates of flow are then repeated back to high tide—the whole process taking approximately 12 hrs 20 mins. High tides, therefore, are about 40 mins later each day.

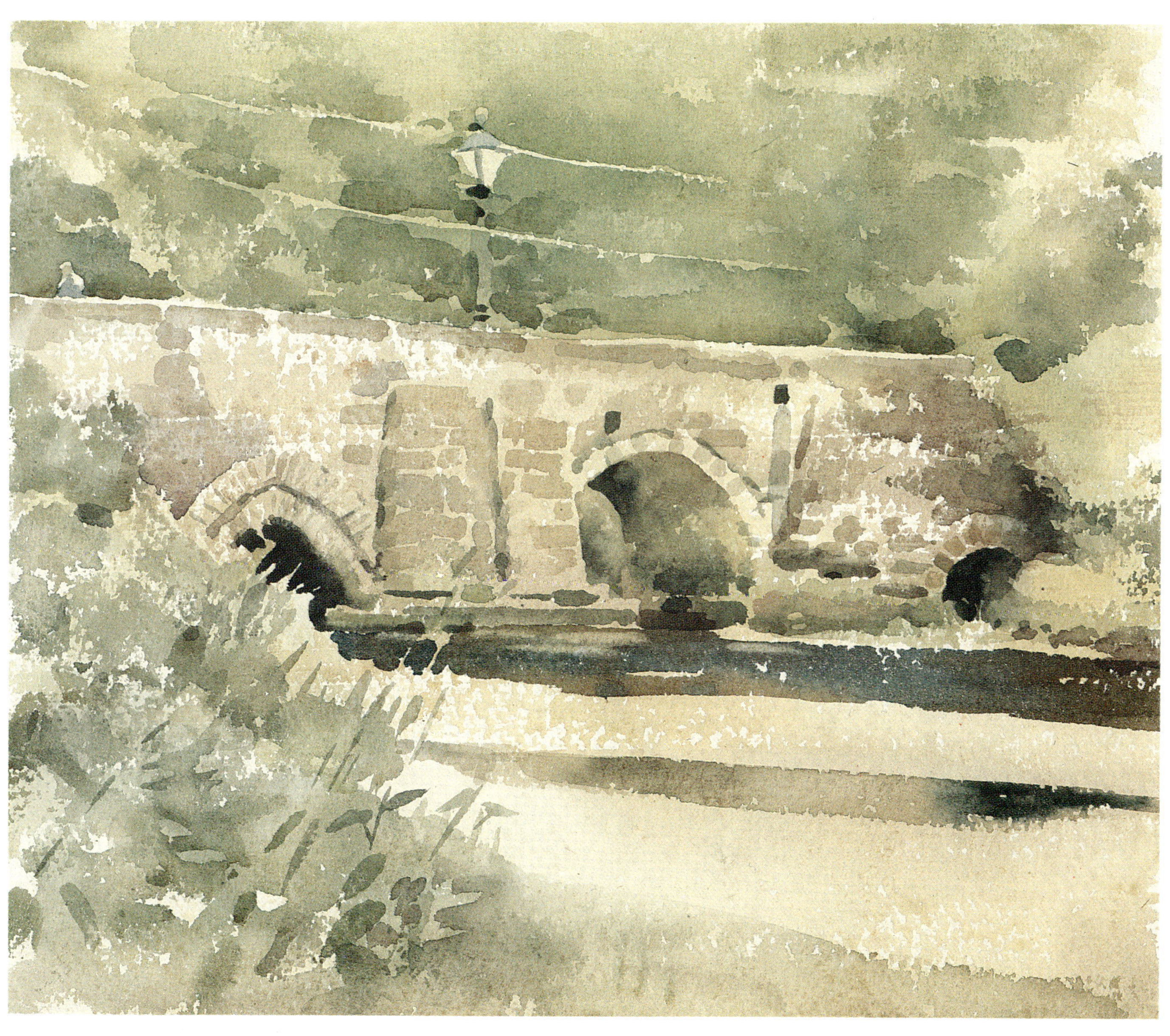

LOSTWITHIEL

'— between showers, I painted the bridge and pool from where I would begin my shakedown journey to Fowey.'

I rearranged things on board so the boat looked less like jetsam. I could lean on the sail-bag, the waterproofs and sleeping bag, but the gaff, boom, easel, wellingtons and buckets were continually in the way. After shipping the oars a few times I found the resulting rivulets running into the boat a nuisance, but after a spot of trial and error found a position on the gunwales where the oars were held securely and drained unwanted water overboard—I was getting used to watery ways.

Two miles further on I saw St Winnow's sunlit church tower above trees, and tied up to a mooring buoy fifty yards upstream. The view over the stern included a varied collection of small craft beached in dark recesses under the trees—I was tempted to attempt painting a watercolour while afloat. I thought it might not be possible from such an unstable platform, hence my initial search for a character boat which I expected would appear in several paintings. My fear was unfounded and I was happy with the result. A steady current kept me facing towards the church, and as I look more at the subject than the painting, my mind remains in the real world and my balance is not affected. On the oars, which I lay across the gunwales, I hung my waterpot and rested my painting and palette. With the sailbag against the mast forming a comfortable backrest, and the warmth of the sun and gentle motion, I was almost too comfortable to work.

On the move again at 4:30. The river, running and dropping quite fast, formed four foot mud walls on the outside bends and wide, almost flat stretches on the inner. I looked up at herons feeding a few feet away as I was rushed by in the deeper water under the mini-cliffs. Carefully standing, I looked with a bird's-eye view into leafy mud floored tunnels between trees. The feathered feeders ignored my head as it whizzed by.

The distance between the banks after St Winnow was up to a quarter of a mile, although the navigable width for boats larger than the Mirror was just a few yards by that time. I wished to travel up the Lerryn River but, as I expected, on reaching the mouth there was very little water—I would soon have been stranded had I entered. A couple of hundred yards further on I picked up a mooring at a spot from where I could make a painting of the river junction. It was about ninety minutes to low water and while painting the boat grounded.

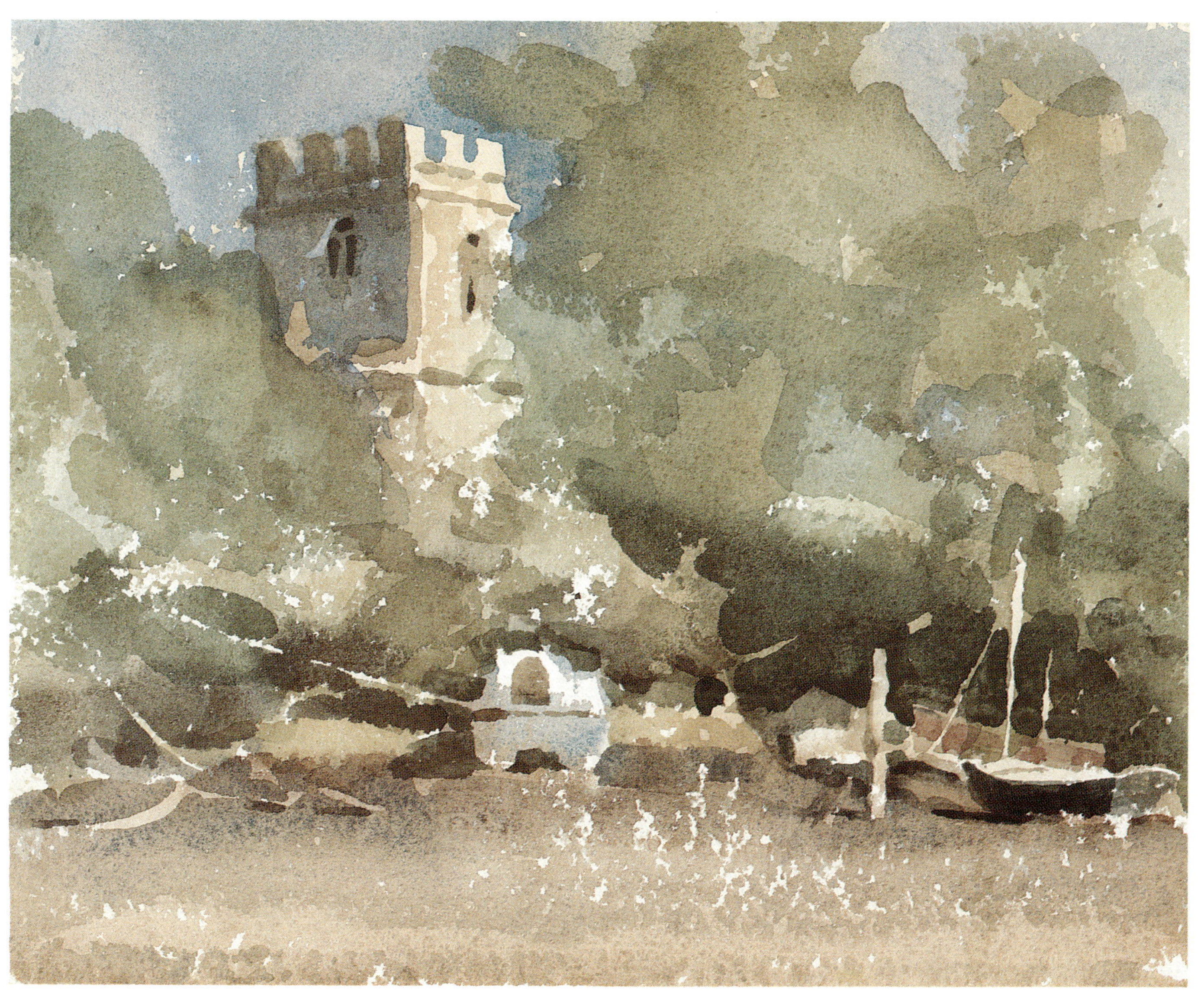

ST. WINNOW

'The view over the stern included a varied collection of small craft beached in dark recesses under the trees – I was tempted to attempt painting a watercolour while afloat.'

At 8:00, accompanied by a squadron of ducks, the slow moving tide eased the dinghy into the little river. The evening was still, and in complete silence, save for a quack or two, my journey continued in growing darkness. Travelling with, and not through the water, I appeared to be stationary, watching a moving landscape of rounded mud banks and their reflections forming a milk chocolate world. The milk became dark, then pitch, and I was relieved when the lights of Lerryn loomed. Bewellied, I slurped up a steep mud bank on the edge of the village, tied a line to a post and proceeded to the Ship Inn. I washed my boots at convenient stepping stones before entering and rejoining the human race. It was 10:00.

One and a half hours later, feeling content, I recrossed a fairy-tale arched bridge that spanned the narrow creek close to where I had tied up. The little boat had been elevated several feet above the mud that made climbing out so awkward, and I was able to step back aboard from the grass in a most civilized manner. There was a trace of rain in the air which stirred ominously and prompted me to don an all-in-one, olive green oilskin suit loaned to me by Mevagissey fisherman Mike (not to be confused with Michael). I noticed prior to landing, faintly illuminated by the distant village lights, a vacant buoy a few yards downriver. In darkness I headed that way, ran into it a few seconds later and made fast.

I had expected to sleep on river banks or beaches, but the night was dark and I felt more at home on the little dinghy. I filled the space between the centreboard case and side buoyancy chamber with my sail and kit bags and buckets. Topping the makeshift bed with the centreboard I had a flattish surface on which to attempt to sleep, and lay down with my head on the foredeck against the mast, and felt quite comfortable.

Within three or four hours I had to be on the move, or become mudbound. In fact I was on the move half an hour later. The lit cottage windows appeared to be circling the boat and I assumed the tide was turning, but soon realized the wind had freshened. As the tempo of my 'trip round the buoy' increased, so did the rain—a few heavy spots at first, followed by a mini monsoon. I quickly covered myself and gear with a polythene sheet, but unfortunately, it was untucked repeatedly by the wind. Before midnight with my face against the plastic, I thought ruefully, how near to a rainless day it had been. Gripping the inadequate covering round my head I peered into the darkness as the spinning lights gradually went out. There were several heavy showers before the boat began to ground at 3:30 when I pushed off into the void. As the wind decreased I rowed blindly but carefully to deeper water. Soon the faint blue/green light of dawn revealed the vague silhouettes of trees and I made my way safely down to the Fowey river.

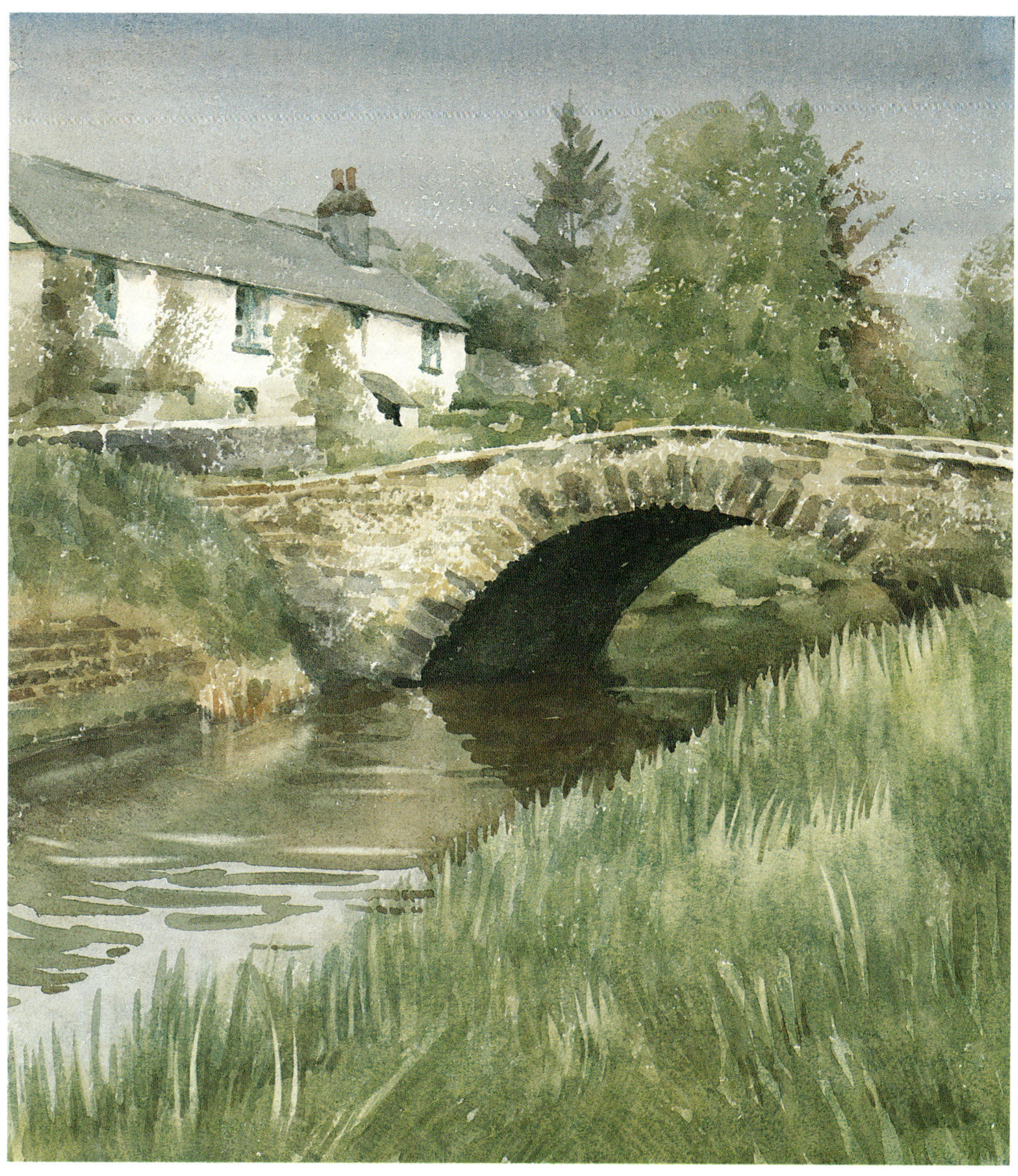

FAIRY-TALE BRIDGE, Lerryn

'– feeling content, I recrossed a fairy-tale arched bridge that spanned the narrow creek close to where I had tied up.'

Fowey harbour begins a mile and a half below the confluence, and Golant, hidden behind a riverside railway embankment, is halfway between the two. From the river, access to Golant is gained by passing under a low railway bridge within a period approximately two hours either side of high tide. Had I been passing later I would have taken down the mast and entered the peaceful retreat. The roadside pub, the Fisherman's Arms, becomes a riverside pub at spring tides, and cars are liable to become semi-submersibles if warning signs are missed or unheeded.*

At around 5:00 I hitched to a mooring near a group of large unoccupied yachts. Two or three hundred yards downstream was a left hand bend which would later lead me into Fowey River Harbour. I found it hard to believe that only sixteen hours had elapsed since launch-time at the bridge pool. Strange also that I had not seen a craft of any description underway during that period. After breakfasting on orange juice and chocolate, I washed, cleaned my teeth and warmed myself in the morning sunshine while soaking up the scenery. A slight breeze caused mirrored masts to distort a little towards their tips, and the ragged edged reflections of trees and fields on the hillsides became indistinct in the misty morning haze further upriver.

I cast off and raised the jib. The smooth, fast flowing river was responsible for most of my progress—the small sail provided steerageway. To starboard ** I passed large ocean-going ships loading at the English China Clay jetties. (Vessels up to 12,000 tons carry clay out of the Fowey River). The scene was a complete contrast to the peaceful upstream riverscape. After rounding the bend I made my way to the slip at Caffa Mill car park—on the west side of the river where Fowey begins and from where a car-ferry crosses to Bodinnick. With the centreboard and rudder removed and standing towards the back to lift the bow, I nudged the little blue boat onto the slip and stepped clear of the water.

The shakedown had gone well. The previous night was just a memory, and I felt sure there wouldn't be another like that—after all it was the end of June.

* Spring tides occur roughly every fifteen days when the rise and fall are greatest. Neap tides are between springs and can be five feet less.

** The jingle—'There's a little red port left', reminds me which side [and colour] of the boat is which when facing the bow.

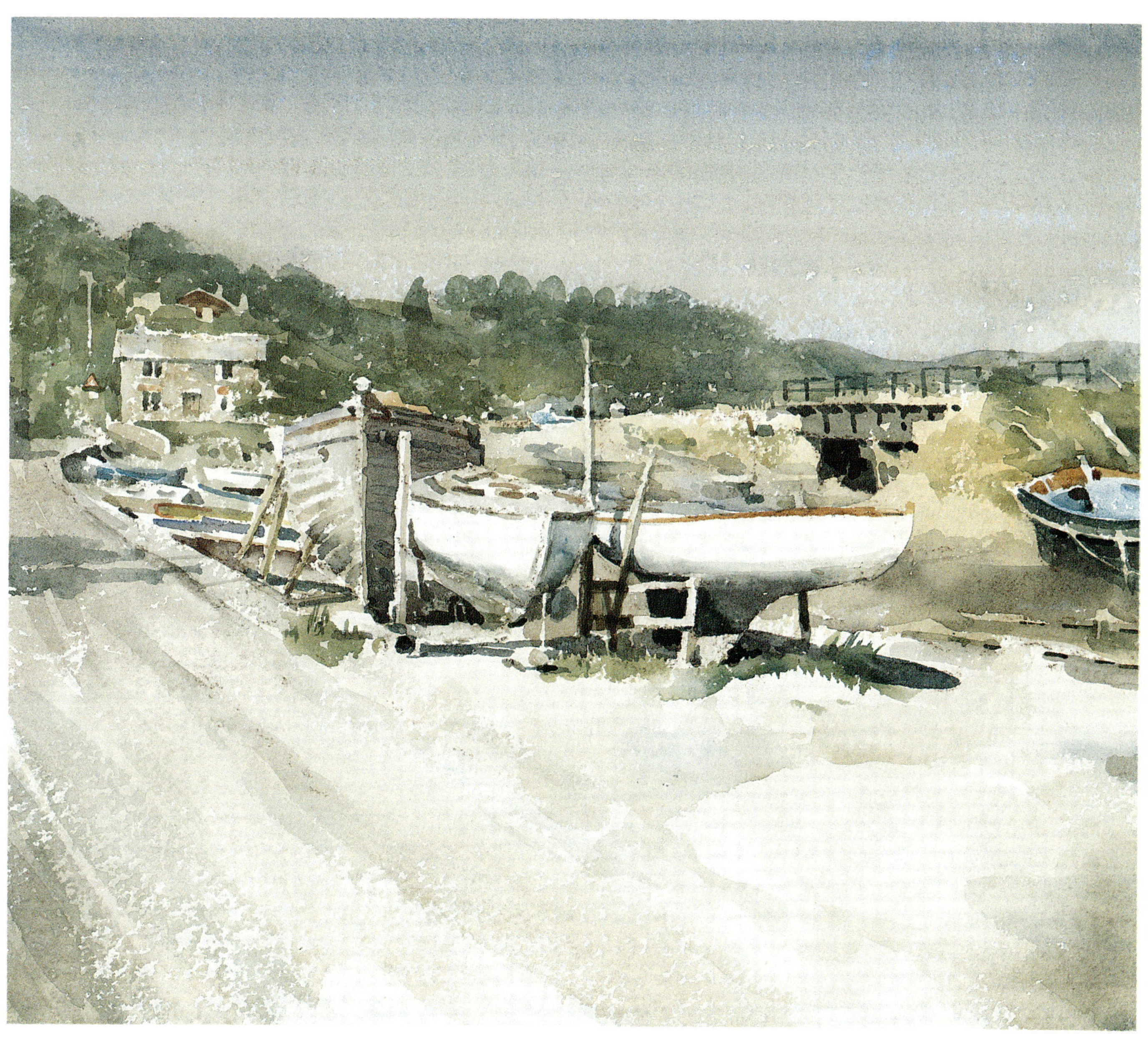

TRIO FOR RENOVATION, Golant

'—access to Golant is gained by passing under a low railway bridge—. Had I been passing later I would have taken down the mast and entered the peaceful retreat.'

Refit

After a roof-rack ride home, the dinghy resumed its rain collection role on the front lawn. While waiting for a change in the weather I carried out a minor refit—though little needed changing. The minimum amount of equipment would be carried on the 'big trip'—so there would be less to go wrong or worry about. On the Fowey River, the gaff (mast extension) and boom (pole on the bottom of the mainsail) were not used—they served as unnecessary deck cargo. On the rivers, extra sail area would rarely be needed so I dispensed with the cumbersome spars and mainsail. If there was little wind I could catch the tide, wait for the next one, or row. It would be too dangerous to carry a top heavy rig when away from help—particularly at sea. And besides, I would be in no hurry.

I borrowed a white jib, similar in size to my red one, which would be used as a loose-footed mainsail. It could be reefed (made smaller) by folding it round the mast. The two sails, hopefully, would enable me to head into the wind. A spinnaker resembling a ten foot bikini cup, for sailing downwind, was among the sails—it induced thoughts of trade winds, flying fish and large mermaids. A small metal cleat was added to the base of the mast to augment two flimsy plastic ones. The pair of six foot six non matching oars had worn quite a bit on the rowlocks, so I covered the damaged areas with leather strips held in place by copper tacks. The oars, a boathook and a small compass were from a previous boat. With the Mirror came a bailer and large sponge. The sponge was a most useful item—so too was the bailer, for which I found a second use! A lidded plastic one gallon ice-cream container would keep dry a notebook, Walkman radio, camera and Elastoplast (a more comprehensive first aid kit would have been in order). Two five gallon plastic lidded buckets held mooring lines, a few tools, assorted shackles, copper nails and sailmaker's needle and thread. Under the foredeck, behind a buoyancy compartment, is a small storage area in which I kept cartons of orange juice, a two gallon water container, a folding anchor and my vintage wellingtons—the right one sporting a non functioning patch.

A plastic survival bag to cocoon my sleeping bag was purchased – a lesson from Lerryn. To protect my finished paintings and painting equipment I carried a few strong plastic bags. The previously mentioned water container was also plastic. Although I think myself as being at one with natural and traditional materials, at times on the trip I not only drank from but lived under, in and on PLASTIC.

The dinghy needed a name. With such circumnavigators as Sir Francis Chichester and Robin Knox-Johnston I had made epic voyages – between book covers. I named the boat Epic with such great sailors in mind, and would be content to cover 359 degrees less than my mentors. Like Chichester, I hoped to sail out of Plymouth Sound; and into Carrick Roads after Knox-Johnston.

The little boat received a name, but was to lose 'that blue' – the colour would not help my paintings. I formed the name on the transom with wide roughly torn masking tape, and after painting the hull sides and stem and stern white, I peeled away the tape to reveal sky blue letters. It was then just a question of waiting for the rain to stop for my 'Epic' voyage to begin.

A Gentle Start

In warm sunshine we parked on high-ground at St Ann's Chapel and tried to pin-point the course of the Tamar and tributaries, but could see only a couple of vague silvery 'lakes' close to the hazy coastline where sea and river met thirteen miles away. It was 10 a.m. on the 5th of July and Toby, my eldest son, was ferrying me to Morwellham Quay. Epic sat on the car inverted like a large sun-hat. The early morning shipping forecast foretold the favourable change and I was eager to find out what mysteries lay hidden in the expanse of inviting wooded valley before us.

On the slip, Epic was dwarfed by Lynher – the last remaining Tamar barge. It was being renovated after salvage from the mud of the Lynher (sometimes called St Germans) River. While rigging and loading, the river crept round Epic's newly painted hull urging the adventure to begin. An hour before high water I pulled away from the slip, waved, then quickly rowed back – I had forgotten to fit the drainage bung. I was pleased my send-off party numbered only one. After re-launching I removed my wellies, hung my right sock on the transom to dry, waved a second farewell to Toby and in a light fitful wind set the jib and headed upriver.

The rare freedom I experienced was tempered by empty pages. Behind me were the weeks of preparation and trepidation – but I found it difficult to relax initially. Virgin sheets of handmade watercolour paper and a pristine spiral-bound note-book reminded me of my mission. My previous little book just happened – notes to accompany the exhibition of Turkish paintings expanded into an illustrated story. This was different – premeditated. On my way up to Weirhead, which was reached at high-water around 1:00, I felt the uneasy sensation ebbing away. The project needed to be performed at nature's pace, to which I gradually adjusted. The tide turned and my journey to the sea began.

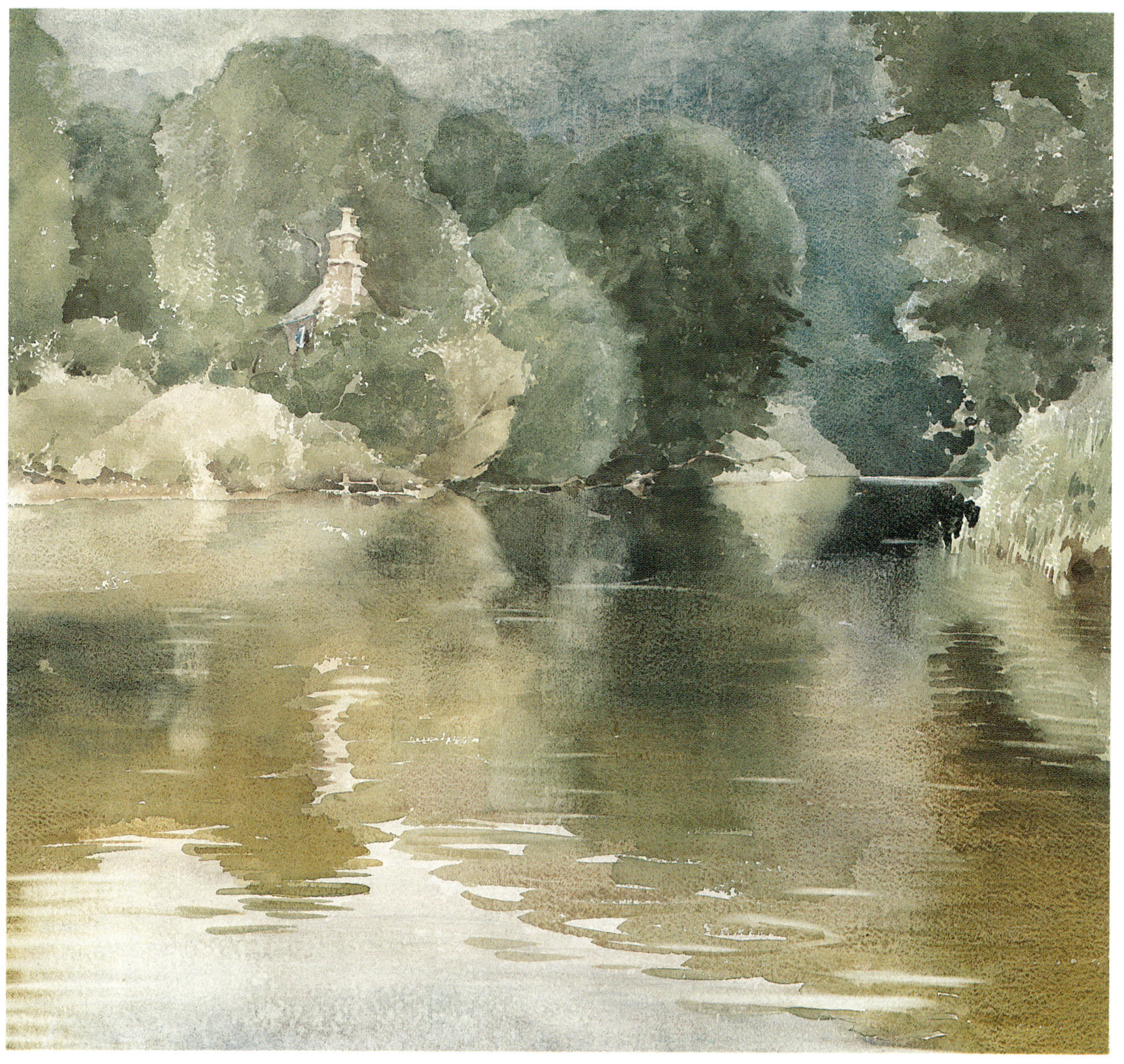

TAMAR COTTAGE

'I rested, listening to soothing guitar music that drifted from a riverside cottage. The banks and trees were very green and the river on which Epic slowly revolved was brimful and coffee coloured after the rains.'

Five hundred yards below the weir a breeze held me almost stationary for a while. I rested, listening to soothing guitar music that drifted from a riverside cottage. The banks and trees were very green and the river on which Epic slowly revolved was brimful and coffee coloured after the rains. Cows in the reeds silently watched as I drifted towards Morwell Wood. Sounds of tiny fish plimping from the water did not spoil the peaceful stillness which led me to day-dream. Perhaps not, from dark recesses, the sparkle of a mole's eye; but definitely, 'derangements' of ducklings, delicate yellow dandelion clocks, fluffing about the river margins.

Nature had restored much of the landscape, tortured during the copper-mining era, but there was still plenty of evidence of the vast scale of the industry. Quays and wharfs, mostly hidden by vegetation, were often in good order—testimony to the skill of early engineers. Back at Morwellham I passed Beatrice Maud (Thames barge) and Garlandstone (merchant ketch), great ore carrying sailing ships now enjoying retirement and enhancing the Great Dock. A little further on I heard the rattle of the mine trucks and through the trees caught a glimpse of visitors being taken back in time, underground.

The noise faded and presently I arrived at a long straight stretch of river. An old mine chimney stood out powerfully above the wooded hilltop horizon—incongruous engineering in a tree dominated landscape. The bright, breeze-rippled river contrasted with the dark woodland. I beheld the subject for a painting.

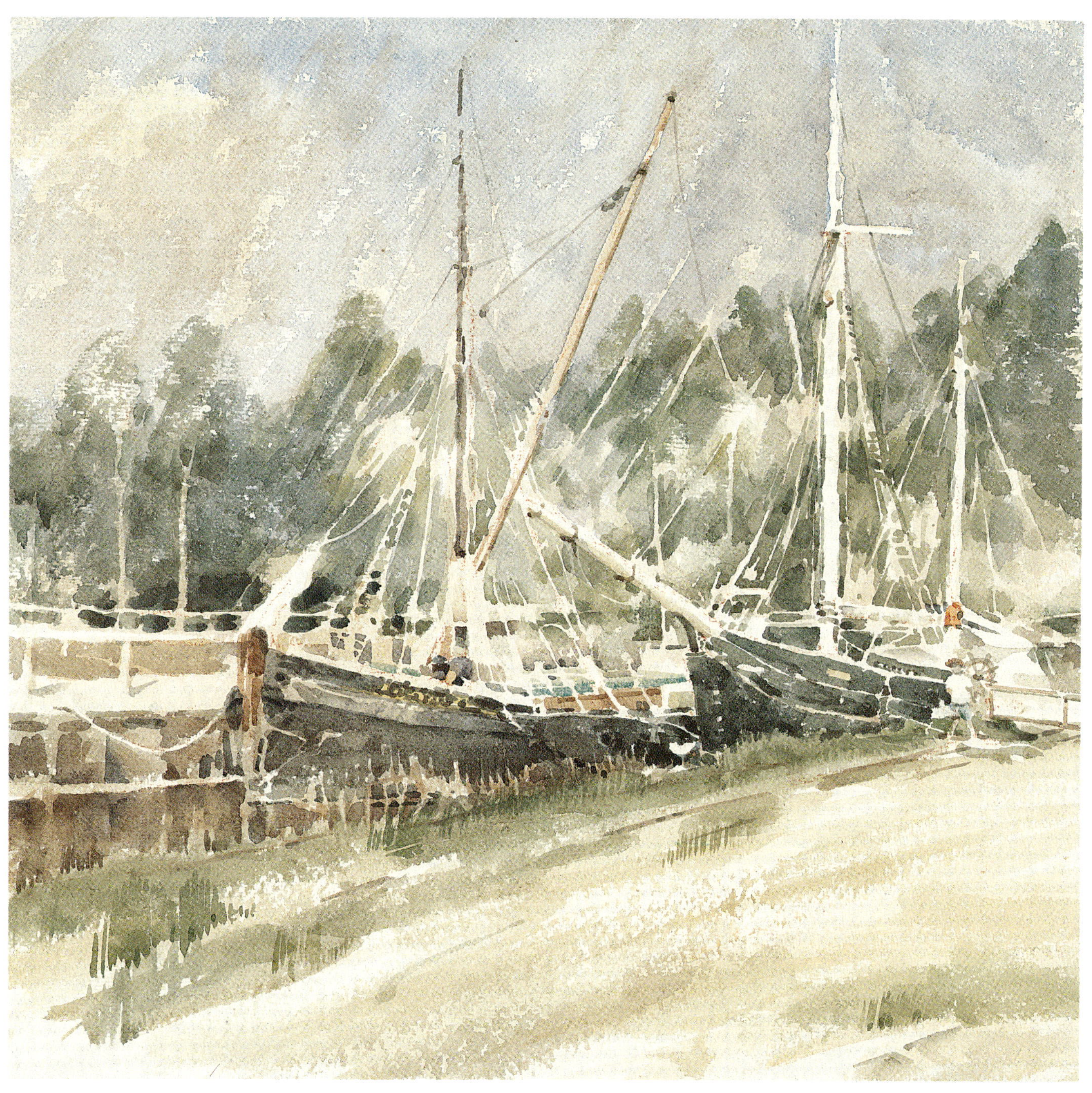

BEATRICE MAUD AND GARLANDSTONE, Morwellham Quay

'—great ore carrying sailing ships now enjoying retirement and enhancing the Great Dock.'

Painting in Mud

Reed beds edged the Cornish side of the river, and to five or six stems I tied Epic. For the following hour or so as I painted, the falling tide repeatedly settled the dinghy on the mud. With an oar I re-floated her, and occasionally lengthened the painter (bow mooring line). Having completed the painting, I whip-snatched the painter to break the boat free. To pull loose a rope tied to a few reeds is quite simple—but not when afloat in a light boat. Epic rushed onto the mud, into which the painter buried itself. My next snatch twanged free the line, showering the scene with mud splashes. Miraculously the painting remained mud-less and I stowed it safely before re-engaging. After a few more attempts, the muddy painter thrashed free the muddy painter leaving a bedraggled Epic and crew on the mud with the river inexorably receding. I escaped my glutinous captor with a session of desperate mud rowing, and returned to the river where I set about Epic with my trusty sponge. As the current hurried me on my way a few oar strokes were needed to counteract the gusty breeze and keep me away from the banks while I cleaned up and tidied away my painting equipment.

It remained warm and became hazy, though a vague sun was discernible from time to time. The mud banks being revealed were of a cocoa or yellow ochrey hue—a surface colour only, for mud lifted on the oar blades was a dead, graphite grey. Occasionally I noticed wooden cruising sailing boats—usually older craft of character, often mothballed—covered by old tarpaulins and afloat only at spring tides. Some were partly hidden in a minicreek or an excavated berth on the fringe of the river. I suppose I missed others that were completely concealed by the undergrowth. They were machines of dreams—waiting to be slipped into adventure on the river, thence to the waterways of the world. Some may never leave the mud—destined to journey only in the winds of romantic dreamers.

Over the trees mysterious old mine chimneys were visible. Some were broken or leaned at 'impossible' angles, and when sighted again from further down-river they had been 'miraculously straightened'.

At 6:00 I picked up a mooring a few hundred yards upriver from Calstock Viaduct which I proceeded to paint. After less than half an hour the tide turned and I had to reposition myself as the boat slowly swung round. In the next thirty minutes or so, as I completed the picture, it became dull and cold and I anticipated a relaxing evening in a local hostelry. While the current was still fairly slack I rowed down to Calstock, and finding access to the town car-park area protected by mud I proceeded a little further and landed on rocks at the bottom of stone steps where I temporarily hitched Epic. I wandered up the little side street where two men were in conversation. From one (Douglas), I was extremely fortunate to be offered the use of the running mooring next to where I had left Epic. I thanked the kind gentleman and returned to tie on to the loop of heavy rope fixed between two pulley-wheels—one fixed by the side of the steps and the other way out on the riverbed. I 'pullied' Epic ten yards into the river where she lay out of harms way to an increasing current, poignantly pointing seawards.

Cowboys and Lightning

As I wandered down to the riverside car-park area I passed a group of cowboys and a sheriff. In the saloon of the Tamar Inn more wild westerners were casually propping up the bar, mindful of their heel wheels. I drank a beer and chilli-concarnied but still felt out of time and place; so I mosied up to the Boot Inn. It was a pleasant pub, peaceful and beamful of character, and not a cowboy in sight. Before I had finished my pint I saw flashing lights—the cosy gloom was shattered by a grand lightning show. I had little time to enjoy the *son et lumiere* for a rain-laden sky brought a premature dusk followed by, '—a few heavy spots at first—'. (Yes, there could be another like that). I hastily finished my pint, raced to the running mooring, 'pullied' in and hurriedly boarded, then as the skies emptied I cast off—obviously carried away by the dramatic turn of events. On reflection, after polythening the contents, I should have left Epic on the mooring and retired to the Boot to continue my 'relaxing evening'.

I rowed out into the fast flowing river and tied to a buoy in mid stream where I spent an interesting half hour under plastic. I watched cow-persons inelegantly clopping on high boot-heels to the shelter of Calstock Social Club from where megatonic, cacophonous country music began to emanate. Darkness descended so I decided to call it a day, and with polythene at the ready, lay down to sleep. The music became ultra megatonic, and as the current had begun to slacken I was able to row to a more peaceful mooring a few hundred yards past the viaduct. I dozed to the sound of distant drums till peace reigned at tide turning. Then, with the wind increasing, I was treated to a series of showers, and by dawn I was quite alarmed—the outgoing stream was at its maximum and a strong wind howled downstream under the viaduct. It was impossible to reach a landing place at Calstock so I waited anxiously for the early shipping forecast at 5:55. Unpleasantness was foretold and I headed down-river knowing I would soon have to temporarily abort the mission before arriving at wider exposed reaches.

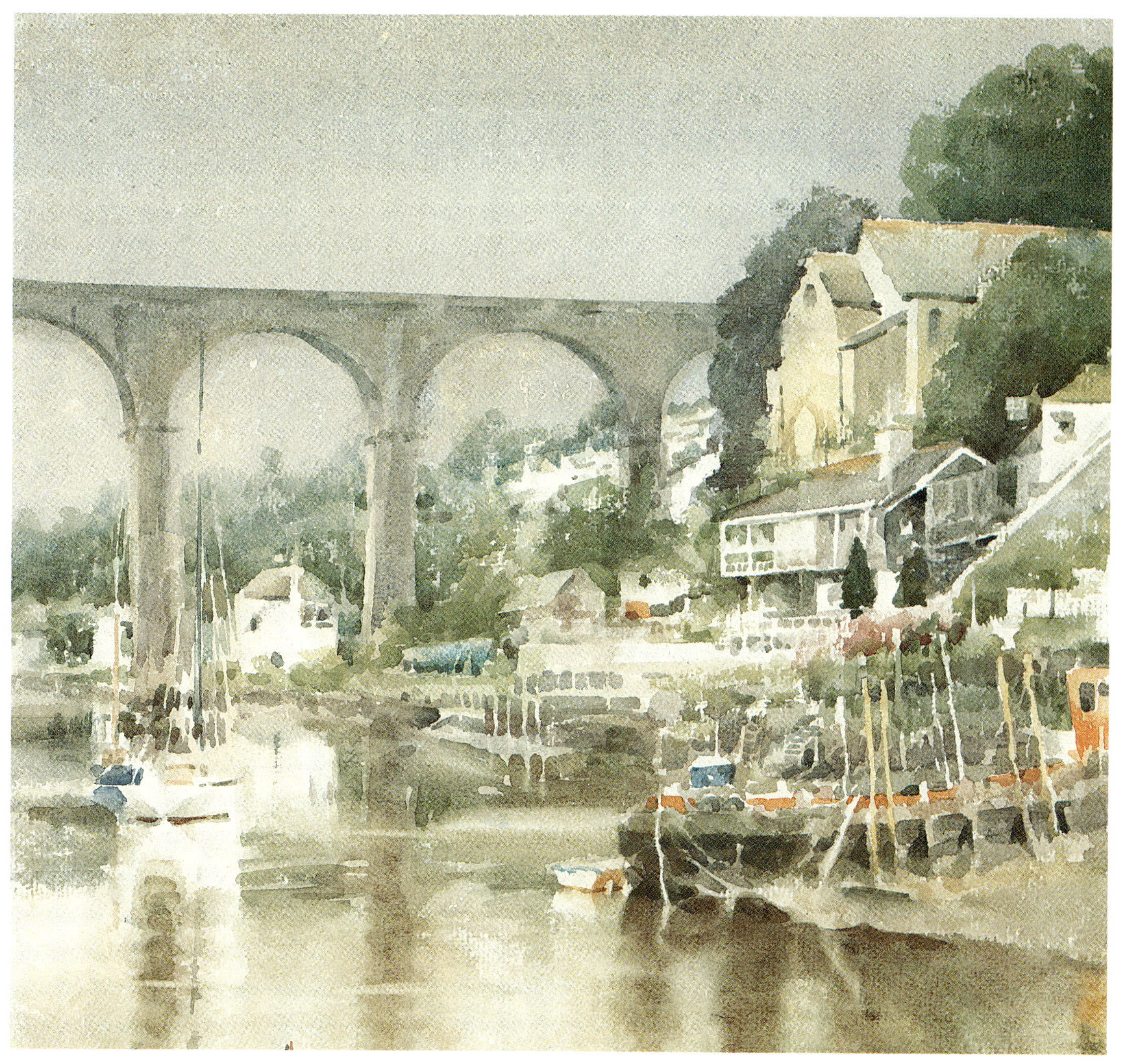

CALSTOCK

I dozed to the sound of distant drums till peace reigned at tide turning.

On the outskirts of town I passed a boatyard and hoped I would not regret so doing—I did not wish to end the leg so soon and ignominiously. Cotehele Quay seemed a more appropriate landing place and was only a mile away. The river of seawater, which had reflected the grey green sky, had been replaced by 'fresh' muddy brown water by the time I reached Cotehele at 7:00—exactly low tide. The windswept river and muddy banks did not lessen the beauty of the imposing group of buildings. Shamrock, the last surviving coastal barge (a powerful workhorse, similar to the rugged Thames barges) was resting in its mud-berth and graced the setting. I detected the form of a slipway beneath the mud and grounded prior to squelching up to a quay wall where I secured a long line. I thought it too early to seek permission for extended parking and took advantage of a spell of rare sunshine to warm my feet. After exploring, I arranged boat storage. While waiting for the river to rise, and Toby to pick me up, I painted a detail of one of the castellated buildings.

As we left Cotehele Quay, a sailing sloop about twenty two feet in length was receiving quite a buffeting as she was taken down-river under power. I would follow when the weather settled. Third time lucky, perhaps.

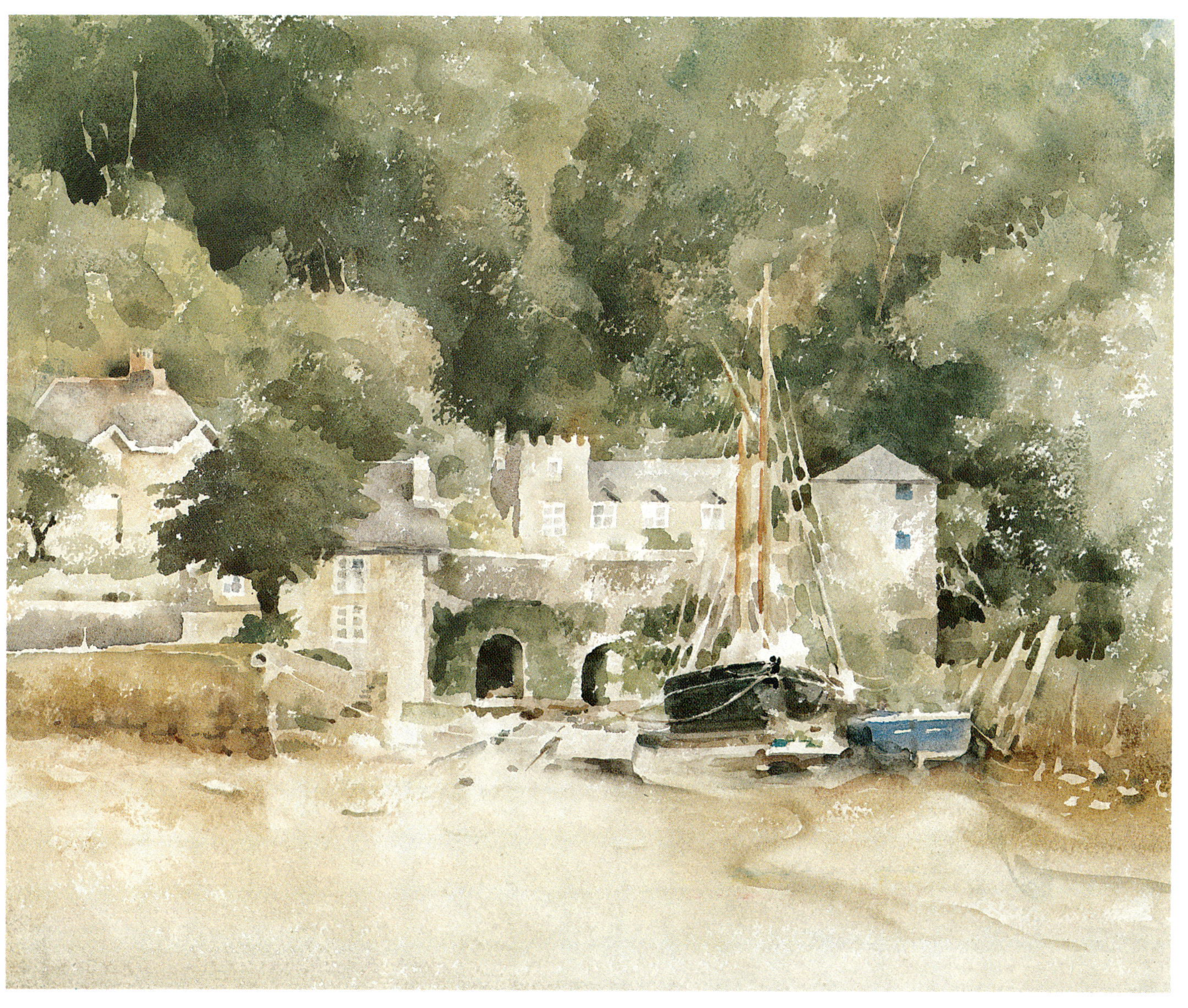

COTEHELE QUAY

'Shamrock, the last surviving coastal barge (a powerful workhorse, similar to the rugged Thames barges) was resting in its mud-berth and graced the setting.'

Get Out And Walk

It rained and blew and I listened to many weather forecasts. July was half over before I returned to Cotehele Quay to be reunited with a damp little Epic, upturned in the boat compound like a picnic table pining for the sun. Toby, who had chauffeured me through the showers, helped me rig and re-clutter the dinghy. We sheltered in the car during a particularly heavy shower, wondering when the 'later', in the weatherman's clearing up later, would begin.

At 10:30, as the river began to fall, I drifted away from Cotehele under black clouds. The spring tide had created sufficient flow to make it very difficult for me to go back to a sign I had failed to notice a few seconds earlier. However, after a couple of minutes aggressive rowing, I was close enough to read, 'DANGER, Hidden Weir 20yds.' and wondered if it was always that well hidden.

The grey clouds lightened as areas of blue increased. Two miles downstream I met Dave who was sitting on the wall at Halton Quay. I stepped ashore on the shingle and chatted to the licensed salmon fisherman. He explained the presence of the rowing boats that I had seen on my way down-river. They were about fifteen feet in length with large painted numbers on their sides. The boats, manned by one or two crew, are to be found on all the rivers that eventually empty into Plymouth Sound. Long nets are stretched across the river at high and low water, when the tides are slack, to snare the majestic game fish. Fishing had steadily worsened, partly due to excess sea fishing, according to Dave, who had caught nothing that morning. Wishing him better luck for the evening session I set the red jib and continued on my way.

Half a mile downstream, below Pentillie Castle which was hidden behind trees high up on the Cornish bank, is a grand boathouse of stone and two-toned tile construction. A gabled, open-sided porch, with the roof resting on four stone columns enhances the down-stream side of the building. I would have liked to paint it, but respected the 'No Landing' sign.

Below the boathouse the river formed a giant 'S'. The first three mile loop almost encircled a portion of Devon. Cornwall's semi-encircled section revealed at low tide a half mile wide mud plateau, which unfortunately became more than a passing interest. On reaching the second bend I appeared to have entered a large lake. Not realizing the average depth was a rapidly decreasing six inches, I failed to keep to the outside of the bend, and my corner cutting cost me dear. What was a floating flotilla of seagulls became a pedestrian flock. Mud flats became discernible and shallow winding channels rapidly drained into the main stream. After a vain attempt to escape down one of the rivulets, I stood up and commenced an over optimistic escape strategy. To take my weight off the boat while I pushed the oars against the mud I half jumped—the net result of those repeated actions, besides progressing an insignificant twenty yards, was to leave tracks that an optimistic zoologist may have later deduced was the spot where a very giant turtle had laid her eggs. In forcing the boat along in the ungainly, strength-sapping mode, I had unknowingly pumped a gallon or so of the glutinous grey up the centre-case, and on reaching total exhaustion I sat down in it. Had it been raining, my tether would have been nigh—but the secretive sun relented, and shining warmingly it filled me with as good a cheer as I could have reasonably expected. I removed my muddy jeans and shirt, donned denim shorts and stepped over the side.

Folk from the hamlets of Hooe and Hole's Hole on the Devon side of the river, had they been following my progress round the bend, may have wondered what entertainment lay ahead. From the moment I settled up to my knees in the mud I think I acquitted myself with distinction. The sensation of cool fine mud oozing between my toes was pleasant and I (rather foolishly) gave no thought to sharp shells as I pushed Epic the hundred yards or so to the edge of the main channel. The flat bottomed boat slipped easily over the mud and provided a firm platform to push down against—saving me from sinking deeper. After reaching the river I was washing one leg when my other foot settled on a smooth object. Holding firmly on to the dinghy I reached down through the mud up to my armpit and carefully extricated an undamaged stemmed wineglass. Had any Hooe'n Hole's Hole people been close enough for me to have held my prize aloft and shouted, 'I've found it', they too may have raised my rating from burk to distinction. On a nearby mooring, in the fast flowing stream, I set about a major clean up of boat, clothes and myself. I was pleased the only lasting evidence of my previous hour's caper was the souvenir from the mud.

The river widened to average half a mile on the two mile stretch from 'mud-corner' to (Cornish) Cargreen where I tied up for lunch. I thought a prolonged restful repast was in order, for I had to wait for the tide to turn before entering the River Tavy. Although quite a large village, Cargreen does not boast a cafe or public conveniences. This is a good thing to ensure continued tranquility for the residents, but not so for a hungry riverfarer with time on his hands.* Seeking sustenance, I made my way up the main street and managed to miss the Supply Store, but noticed it on my return. Time had also passed by the little shop. I entered and stepped back half a century. Many layers of paint covered the sparsely stocked shelves, and the floor was cosily covered with carpets. I purchased from the pleasant little old lady, a few tomatoes, a piece of cheese wired from the block and a packet of Ryvita. I was grateful for the existence of the old time emporium and returned to the river with my victuals.

It was an hour and a half to low water and I drifted on down-river partaking my simple fare. Though still over two miles away I glimpsed for the first time, while afloat, the new Tamar Bridge with Brunell's earlier masterpiece behind. Presently, the impressive multispanned rail bridge that crosses the mouth of the River Tavy hove in view. Whilst enjoying the spectacle of the bridges I heard the telltale swishing sound of disturbed gravel on the hull—it was the sound that preceded my previous grounding. The vast mud spit clearly defined on my map should have been sufficient warning to prevent a recurrence. Even my frantic rowing towards deeper water failed to save me from running aground, again.

The river receded, leaving Epic on the slight ridge that had prevented our escape. Content to remain beached till after low water, I lay down in the bottom of the boat to shelter from the cool wind and rest for an hour. Around 5:00 I stepped on to the firm gritty mud, pushed Epic a few yards to the water and sailed away from my ultimate destination—I headed up the River Tavy into Devonshire.

* I may have been too close to the bank to notice The Spaniards Inn (as large as a liner) on my arrival. The roadside aspect had the appearance of a picturesque half-timbered cottage. Even if the sign, at the time, was being replaced, it was still a shame that my 'innstincts' let me down.

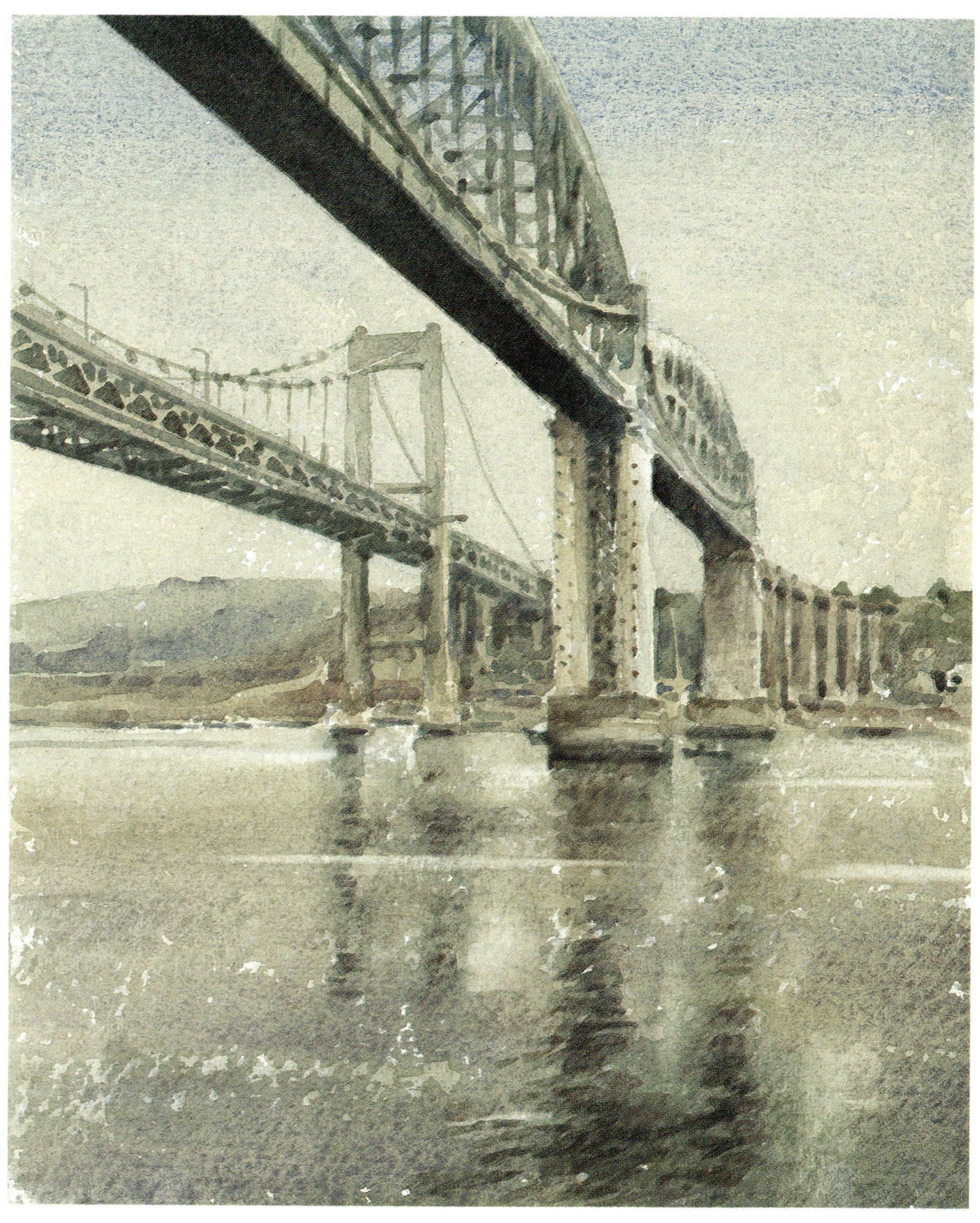

TAMAR BRIDGES

Devon Interlude

To starboard, half a mile past the bridge, I glimpsed between trees a small section of a building on the high tide-line. I pulled in to the rock and kelp festooned foreshore. Although lumpy and extremely slippery, the 'assault course' beach was relatively level and soon to be submerged, so I carried out a tethering manoeuvre – looping a long line over a rock high on the bank. Investigating, I found a somewhat neglected old boat house. The overgrown and much weathered building, standing in the grounds of Warleigh House, was an ideal subject for a painting – but the light was fading so I gave it a miss. Before returning to cast off, I stopped to appreciate a stunning panorama – a complete contrast to the intimate boathouse scene. Epic, seeming so vulnerable and tiny at the edge of the wide waterway was dwarfed by the Tavy Bridge – silhouetted against a dramatic duskening sky. The sun, hidden from me by clouds at that moment, flashed the estuary with silvery light. To capture the glowing luminosity of such a landscape, it would have to be painted on a transparent surface lit from behind.

On the other side of the river and a further mile upstream I passed the church tower dominated village of Bere Ferrers – protected by a mud barrier two to three hundred yards wide. Access was prevented for a couple of hours so I sailed on. I crossed the river to get a clearer view of a small circular castellated tower near Mount Jessop. The fortification is at a point where the river narrows to fifty yards before winding between wooded banks up to Lopwell Dam a mile away.

I tied Epic to railings above a slip-way close to the dam and left her on a rising tide. Three young men were fishing nearby – no locked gates at that weir-pool. With Liverpudlian accent they said they would keep an eye on the dinghy while I went 'hunting'. I asked a passing gentleman for inn locations, then set off to follow his complicated directions. I was pleasantly surprised a few minutes later, when the gentleman, as motorist with family, transported me post haste to the 16th century 'Who'd Have Thought It Inn' at Milton Combe. In a welcoming old world atmosphere, my supper was enhanced by a couple of memorable pints that disappeared as easily as the name of the brew has slipped from my mind – I must return for research purposes.

I walked back to Lopwell through two miles of peaceful pine-forests and rejoined the angling trio. They had enjoyed good sport and were unhooking an eel as I thanked them for boat-sitting. On the risen river, I headed back in near darkness towards Bere Ferrers. Speeding away from Lopwell, on a mirror-like surface, I thought I heard distant shouting above the sound of rattling rowlocks. Then again a few minutes later—sounded Liverpudlian. I ceased rowing and in the gloom noticed a figure running towards the river. Recognizing one of my Mirror minders waving to attract my attention, I glided in through reeds to the grassy bank and was presented with my painting bag by a saviour in a state of near collapse. The bag that had been left on the slip contained my camera and radio; but the most precious item returned was the collection of squirrel-hair brushes in an old cardboard tube. The cylinder, now rather tatty, and some of the brushes, I had taken with me on my first painting trip ten years before. The Scouse Samaritan soon revived and set off with my fervent thanks and a small token for a round of drinks. I was to join him in spirit from The Old Plough Inn, Bere Ferrers, within the half hour—I had to recover from the shock of my good fortune!

At 11:00pm, fully recovered, I stepped into the boat from the quay wall and under oar power headed into the calm darkness—before the river sank below the mud banks and prevented my leaving.

Rhythmic rowing induced sleepy-mind wandering.

There were stars at first as I made my way with the tide to the Tamar.
They faded as I entered a vast endless cave
where sounds of oar-blade splashes echoed against night walls.
Floating dark on black the giant rail-bridge stole over me,
returning me to earth-time.'

A few minutes later, as I left the Tavy, I saw the lights of the Tamar Bridge. The car-deck, decorated with moving headlights, was the sole structured feature amidst the random lights that lay ahead. The bridge was a mile and a half away and rowing to a buoy a hundred yards upriver on the Saltash side seemed to take hours. In fact, between leaving Bere Ferrers and taking up swinging night-time residency in the quick flowing tide, just two hours had elapsed, including an energetic ten minutes locating and catching the vacant mooring. In darkness, the swiftly flowing Tamar carried me past a couple of buoys – I saw them at the last second before they were swallowed by the night. Rowing upstream I still lost way against the emptying river but gained time to grab an elusive float.

Securely hitched, Epic swung from side to side in the outgoing stream. Sleeping bagged I lay down, and with the sound of rushing water spasmodically 'over-ridden' by traffic noise, I attempted to sleep. A few lights were still on in Saltash homes and their close proximity somehow emphasized my bizarre situation.

Somewhat tired, I floated in a metaphysical as well as a nautical sense and the feeling of unreality gave free reign to the wandering of my 'other mind'. Around 3:00, from my exceptionally low vantage point, *'I gazed at a frogman's masked head! It was two or three yards away and only vaguely discernible in the gloom. The helmet moved slowly towards Epic. I kept very still'.* Drifting out of semi-sleep I wondered – some drug smuggling activity, perhaps? When my full powers of reasoning returned I realized I was in imminent danger of being left high and mudbound. Epic making contact with the river-bed had released me from my reverie – not a rubber-suited assassin. There was not sufficient water to submerge a frog, let alone a man. I had been frightened by a mooring buoy and a loop of rope.

I cast off and used the dregs of the outgoing tide to assist me to the mouth of the Lynher River – a mile away. As I negotiated my way between millions of pounds worth of tall masted pleasure craft that lined the river's edge, the eerie stillness was shattered by the 'three thirty' rattling overhead on Isambard's mega-mechano. A little later a powerful pilot boat throbbed up channel and I rode the resulting swells to the sound of halyards flapping against aluminium spars. Silence returned. I ghosted to the mouth of the Lynher to doze away an hour or so till dawn – with Epic tied to a 'frogman's head'.

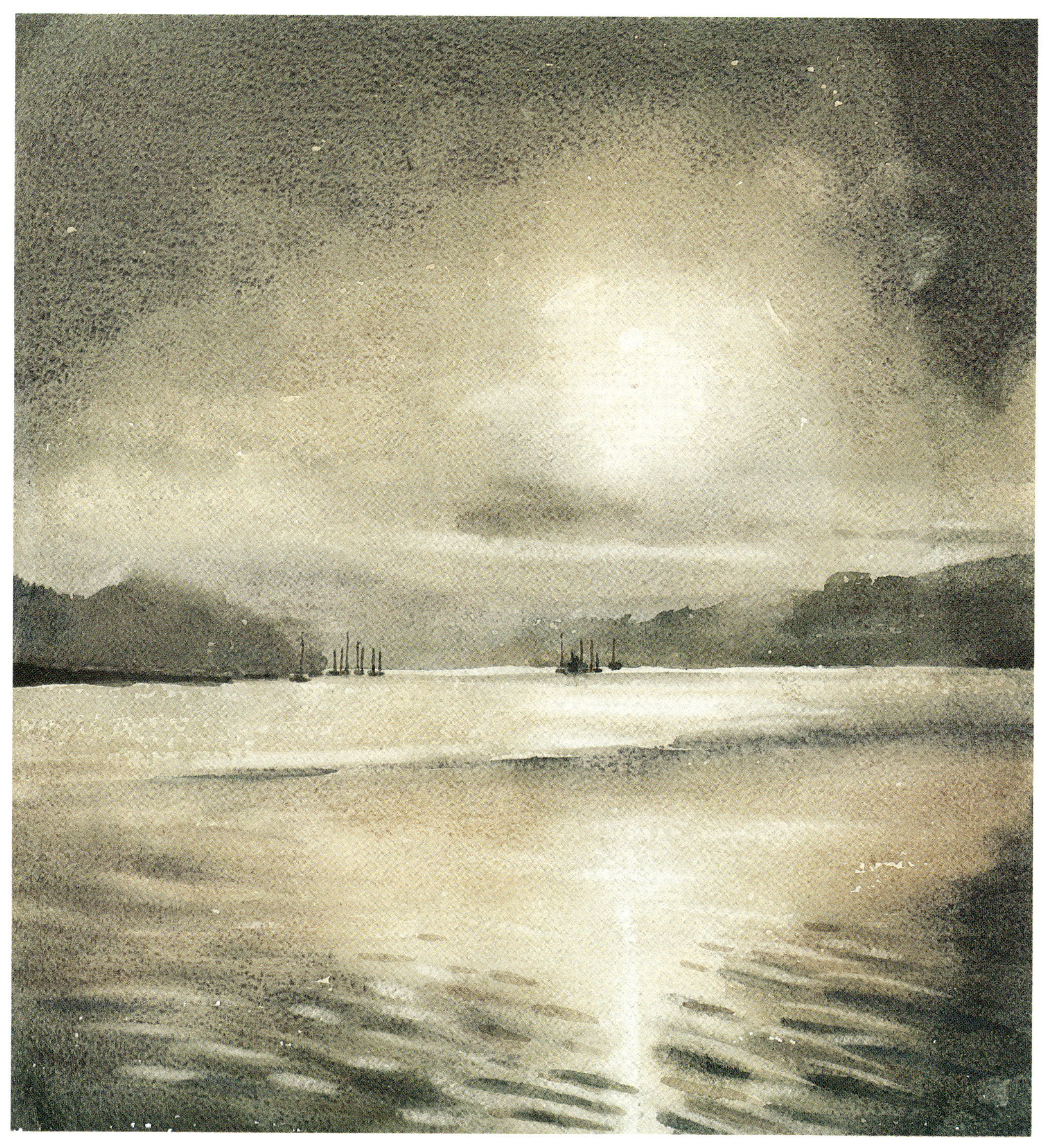

FOG LIFTING ON THE LYNHER

'The fog became low cloud, and fine sunny periods ensued.'

Fog, Ferries and Barbican Bacon

Low tide was just after 5:00. As I was preparing for a tidal ride up to St Germans a bank of fog rolled down the Tamar engulfing the bridges – save for the concrete tower-tops of the road bridge. Gently rowing in the bright stillness, I enjoyed the warmth of the newly risen sun for ten minutes or so before being enveloped in a cold, thickening fog. To starboard, Antony Passage was just visible and I rowed over to the mouth to allow the tide to float me into another world of mud. From the creek entrance I could see the ghostly mass of the railway viaduct four hundred yards away. When I reached the archways they were still barely discernible – the fog had closed right in. The creek was flooding quickly and it was a hard pull back to the river where I was immediately pea-souped. I knew the current was favourable for my purpose and imagined progress as Epic and our little patch of water drifted upstream. Soon a small fog-grey naval ship, tethered between large mooring drums, materialised. (It was large from my point of view). Within ten yards my private little world excluded the ghostly vessel and I continued to examine the 'nothing' as intently as I had the beautiful landscape it concealed. A leaping salmon, perhaps five pounds in weight, came close to joining me in the boat and I wondered how Dave was faring. There were many loud calls and shrieks from birds whose volume seemed to increase in the fog. When three miles up-river, at around 9:00, the visibility slightly improved. I used my compass to determine the correct heading – in the foggy confusion I had entered a creek near Antony (not to be confused with the previous Antony [with] Passage).

The fog became low cloud, and fine sunny periods ensued. With a faint following wind I set my sails goose-winged – one each side, and breezed up to St Germans. On the bank ahead I saw a couple of large sailing boats and one or two dinghies. It was a little before high water and I landed at Tom Cradick's yard. I realised that casual sailors were not really catered for, and at that moment the boss arrived in a large lorry. He could have sent me off to check out the yacht club round the corner (I did not know it was there) but before informing me of its location he said I was welcome to leave Epic at his yard for a day or two. A fresh wind was forecast, making me reluctant to head seaward on that tide. Plymouth Sound could wait a while.

With an hour to spare before the mud would make landing difficult, I stepped back in the boat and sailed a further mile up the Lynher to explore more of the pleasant countryside. I passed under the viaduct and by the well-tended grounds of Port Eliot. On my return I visited the yacht club, landing on a fine concrete slipway—the use of which would not have limited my eventual departure time to high tide.

A pleasant chap pointed out a gentleman who may have been able to help. I waited for him to come alongside the jetty in his large boat to pick up passengers and asked if it were possible to pay for short term parking. The correct procedure was to phone first, he informed me. I explained my situation, but the correct procedure was still to phone. I thanked him (not too sincerely), mentally clicking my heels, and went round to Tom's.

Although keen to restart I had to wait for the weather to settle down. A few days later at high tide early in the afternoon, Robin our middle son notched up an hour's driving practice as he transported Julia and myself to St Germans. After helping me put Epic in the water and before re-stowing, we went for a little row during which he demonstrated his technique of running aground. The 'L' plates on the car were magnetic and would not have stuck to Epic. At 4:15, after thanking Tom and his son (sincerely), I waved goodbye to Julia and Robin, raised both jibs and headed for Plymouth.

I enjoyed a fine sail back down to the mouth of the Lynher. Epic cut through the water in a most exhilarating fashion at times. The river surface was comparatively flat and I was able to head well into the wind. Visibility was good and I enjoyed the bits that were 'mist' on my way up. The cloud cover began to break up heralding a mostly sunny evening. A moderate wind was blowing upstream which roughened the surface and hindered my progress, necessitating repeated tacks across Hamoaze (the lower Tamar stretch from the Lynher to the Sound). I was to travel ten miles, criss-crossing the half mile wide waterway, before passing Devils Point—a little over three miles away. It was an interesting area in which to be delayed. Warships lined the Devon side (Devonport), a sombre contrast to the romantic three-masted barquentine moored mid channel. Sleek ocean sailing cruisers beat powerfully and pointed close to the wind, or ran strongly before it. Epic ambled on. At the Torpoint ferry crossing I assisted the sails with oar-power. Had I not, a rendezvous with the Devon bound ferry would have been touch and go—and perhaps more touch from the Cornwall bound twin which completed the pincer movement.

The wind gradually freshened, on the nose, creating small choppy waves, and it was with relief that I rounded Devil's Point and entered the Sound. It was dark and Drake's Island was just discernible. With the oars shipped Mill Bay Docks was left behind, but within minutes the wind died. I hurriedly rowed a further mile, past The Hoe, The Citadel and round to the Barbican where I tied up alongside the Mayflower Steps, twenty minutes before closing time.

The Admiral MacBride beckoned across the cobbles, and to there I retired to refresh my inner self. I popped out occasionally to check that Epic was safe. She was floating at the end of an excessively thick white rope tied from the bow to a steel ring near the top of the stone steps. The ring was higher than the mast-top, giving Epic the appearance of a toy boat on a piece of string. It seemed most unlikely that the steps would be used again that night for it was dark and quiet. With my mind on Captain Jasper's grilled bacon rolls I glanced out of the window and sustenance became secondary. A multi-decked, extravagantly lit vessel was disgorging happy passengers from where Epic should have been. I was relieved to find my midget sailer safe—the long piece of 'string' had allowed her to be safely shunted aside. Apparently, the unlikely happens at the Mayflower Steps.

On leaving the pub I wandered down to the Captain's stall of gastronomic delights—situated outside the Fishmarket and graced with a mechanical flapping seagull. I ordered thick rashers of bacon in half a French loaf and completed my late elevenses with a mug of tea. Cap'n Jasper's is open all week for all but the first quarter of each day. For creating such an oasis, Jasper (John) should be promoted—to at least equal the rank of MacBride. *(The Cap'n told me at a later date how the business started. As an attraction at a regatta in 1978 he designed a hand-cart. Planning was required—dimensions were generous—opportunity was seized and the cart became an immovable stall. The original idea, selling grilled mini dabs [small, cheap flatfish] in a bun, floundered—three hands were required to cope with the bony dab, paper and plate. The bacon bap saved the day, and is now joined by dozens of delectable savouries).*

I rejoined Epic at the historic steps and rowed out to find a mooring in the mouth of the River Plym. I gave no thought to the Pilgrim Fathers who sailed from the same spot—I was a little anxious regarding my own imminent English Channel confrontation.

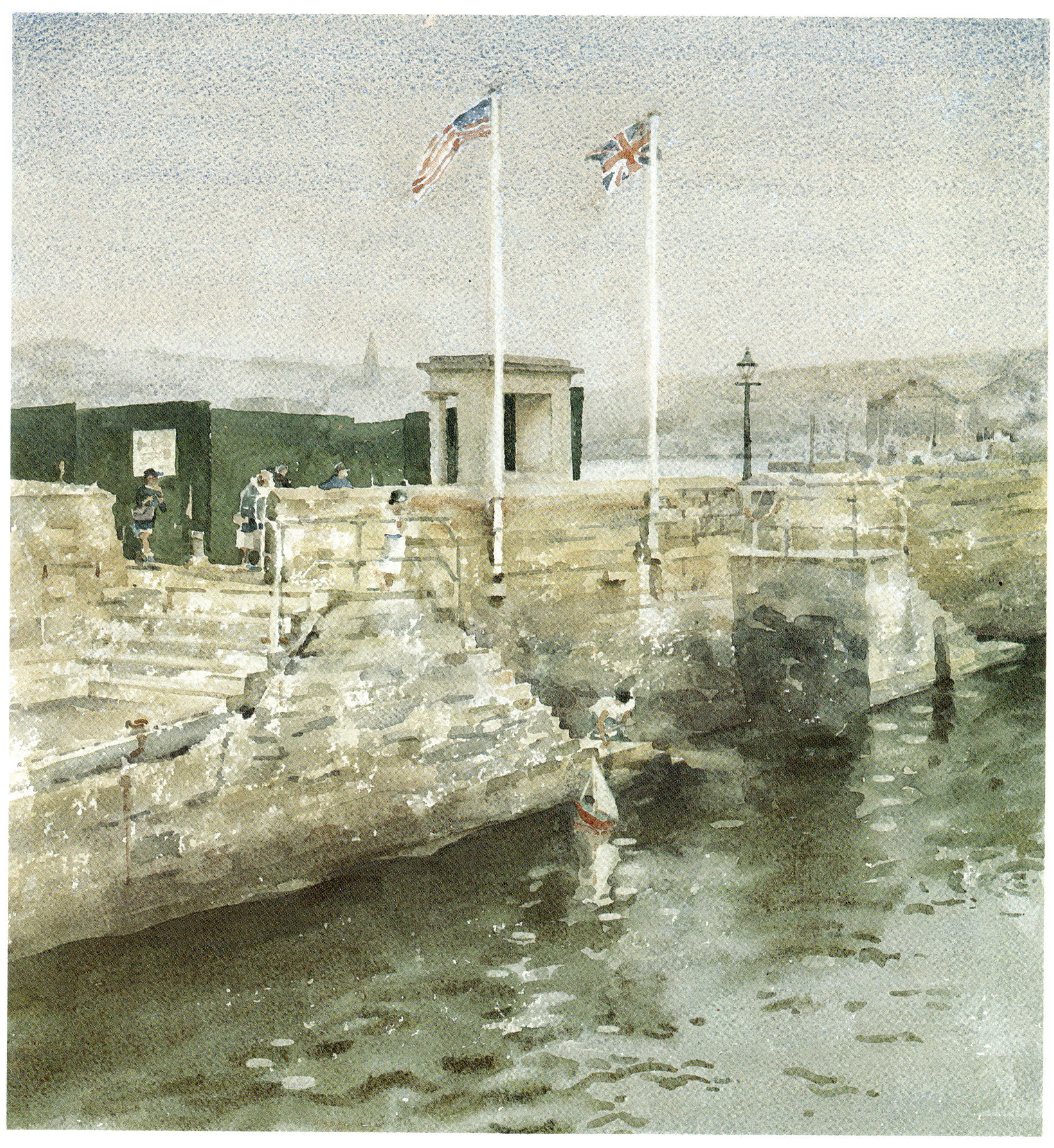

MAYFLOWER STEPS, Barbican, Plymouth

'I hurriedly rowed a further mile, past The Hoe, The Citadel and round to the Barbican where I tied up alongside the Mayflower Steps, twenty minutes before closing time.'

And so to Sea

I felt I had slept a very short while when I peered out of my sleeping-bag at the soft light of the new day. When clearing the decks in preparation for departure, I glanced round and was amazed to find, that apart from a few winking red and green navigation lights, it was pitch dark. The reason for my aberration 'dawned'—I had woken facing the glow of Plymouth's night lights. I lay down to rest for a further hour or so in the half-light. It was still dark (seawards) at 4:30, when under jib I sailed out to the lee of Drake's Island to await the shipping forecast. Epic was hitched to a giant 'Gouda'—a sure sign serious shipping lanes had been reached. Behind me were the smaller, rounder, redder 'Edams'—much used on the rivers. A fine rain washed in the bona fide dawn and revealed, thirty yards away, a twenty four foot, solid looking gaff cutter moored to an identical cheese. The black painted Black Velvet was a boat ideally suited for the next part of my voyage, and Epic was about the right size for the tender.

Penlee Point, where the sea proper begins, was just visible through the gloomy mist between a low part of the western end of Drake's Island and Picklecombe Point. It was three miles away to the south west—the direction from which the wind was blowing. At 6:00, I headed into the drizzly Sound towards Plymouth Breakwater with the words and melody of—'Er lee won moor or ning, jus tas the sun was ri i zing ——' repeating in the back of my mind. (It was one of the medley that preceded the early morning shipping forecasts). My front-line thoughts were evaluating, '—— south westerly three to four, increasing five later. Showers; moderate; fog patches ——'. Force four I thought might be alright, and optimistically decided to carry on for a while—I could always run back to the Barbican if the situation worsened. An engine noise caused me to turn round and behold a huge Brittany Ferry which had crept up on me from behind Drake's Island. Fifteen minutes earlier it had been at sea—it would take me a little longer.

Intermittent rain showers marred an interesting sail out of the Sound. Tacking caused me to pass close by Picklecombe Fort, a large five storey, semi-circular, former fortress on the Cornish side of the Sound. It now contains many luxury apartments, and looked somewhat forbidding at that early grey hour. After a tack out towards the mile long breakwater, I continued into Cawsand Bay from where I inspected Kingsand and Cawsand. They looked as one from the sea and were dominated by Cawsand Fort. It was receiving the Picklecombe treatment—more luxury apartments. I would have liked to call at the 'King- and Caw- sands', but I had an urgent appointment with Rame Head.

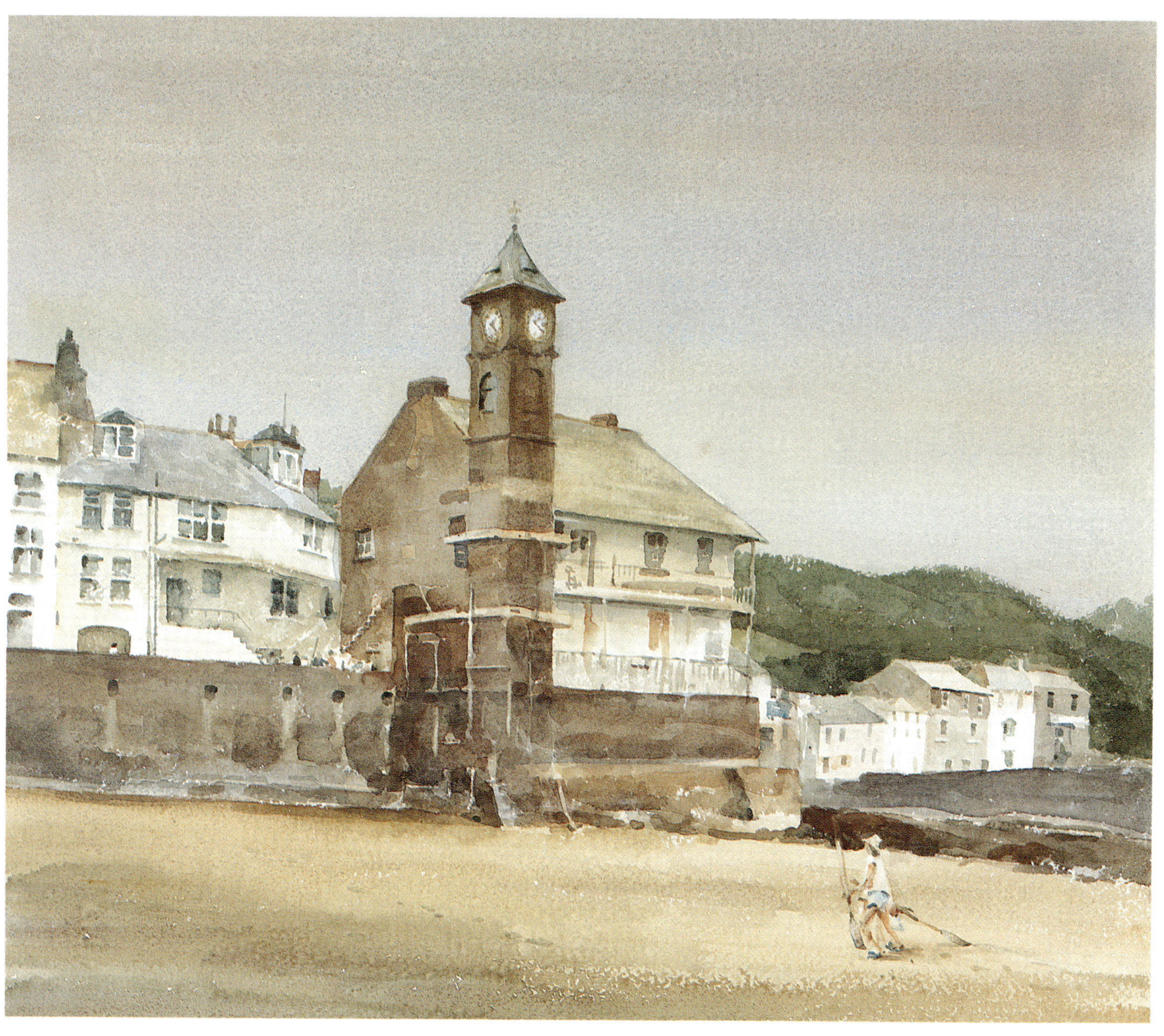

KINGSAND

'I would have liked to call at the 'King- and Caw- sands', but I had an urgent appointment with Rame Head.

After four or five more tacks through a choppy sea I reached Penlee Point and turned westwards. Out in the Channel the motion had changed. Epic elegantly rose over the rounded swells but found some of the waves between tended to alter her heading adversely. Rame Head, the more southerly tip of the promontory, was still a mile and a half away. My course from the Barbican to Rame, measured in straight lines was over six miles and by the time I had put in another series of tacks I must have travelled over twice that distance. The high ground behind Rame was veiled in mist, and as I struggled over a depressing grey sea to reach Whitsand Bay and a favourable wind, I wondered if the coast guard look-out was manned—cut-backs were being made. As I neared the headland the skies cleared, the wind eased and the sun broke through, lifting my spirits.

Thoughts of retreating ceased and I was able to relax. Turning the corner put the wind abeam—the easiest and most beneficial angle for sailing. I slackened the sheets*, and leaning against the mast steered with my feet, drank fresh orange juice and surveyed the scene. Long Sands, a four mile long beach was a mile and a half away and as the wind reduced to a waft I angled in to view the coastline more clearly. I was sedately cruising along, facing the way I had come, when six feet to port a large black fin appeared. Alarm was followed a second later by excitement. The fin was about two feet high, narrower than the classic shark shape and curved over slightly towards the tip. It protruded from the hefty pale grey back of a dolphin which submerged after a few seconds, reappeared twice at ten yard intervals, then disappeared in the direction of Plymouth. I thought they were wont to play around boats for a while, communicating and being patted. I felt slightly slighted.

* The control lines from the loose corners of the sails.

A Little Port to Starboard

After an enjoyable hour sailing past many wooden holiday homes which clung to the steep brackened cliffs I sensed a slight acceleration. Sitting up I paid attention. Freathy village was to starboard, and off to port cloud cover was returning. When about six hundred yards from the shoreline I tightened the sheets, which enabled me to sail parallel to the beach. The wind then met Epic a little forward of the port beam. She began to run into the waves which gradually increased in size and formed small breaking crests. I became used to steering into the larger waves at the last second – this prevented the boat being pushed towards the beach and taking extra water over the side. By degrees the wind-strength increased, and from enjoying an exhilarating sail I feared an overwhelming . . . fear of being overwhelmed.

I sat in the bottom of the boat tight against the windward gunwale which I gripped firmly with my left hand. My weight helped conteract the considerable wind pressure on the sails but unfortunately allowed an unhealthy amount of English Channel aboard. Rame Head was three miles astern when I looked back, but I saw only a mile of foam edged beach and a bank of sinister black cloud. It was too late to run for shelter behind the hidden headland. Visibility decreased further as heavy slanting rain added to the noise of the rapid flapping of the sails' rear edges. Epic sank into troughs and I looked up at awful slabs of water that formed a brief horizon. Occasionally she fell off a wave top and crashed shudderingly down on her flat bottom and I imagined the imminent breakup of the thin plywood hull. At times cross waves met and threw up pyramids of confused sea – more than enough to fill the Mirror which was designed for leisure, not lunatic purposes.

When Rame Head was four miles distant I reached crisis point. Despite my efforts to maintain sea-room, I had been relentlessly driven to within two hundred yards of the beach. Long Stone was visible through the mist just over a mile away. It stood like a ghostly giant tombstone, 'angry white' around its base. (It is sixty feet high and stands two hundred yards off-shore). A short distance before the monolith the rocky shore steps slightly seaward, and my course would have taken me to those ragged cliffs in the lee of the handy monument.

It was too late to make a crash landing on the beach, for Long Sands was astern, replaced by ragged rocks. A hundred yards ahead a small white boat appeared for a second*. I saw it again as it punched through the waves. RESCUE, I thought, though I could not believe it—which was just as well for it disappeared out to sea. (It did not occur to me at the time, that the 'white boat of Tantalus' must have come from somewhere).

Through the spray, a minute later, I saw a patch of beach protected by jagged rock teeth. As the surges receded more rocks appeared—they seemed designed for plywood piercing. I decided in those few seconds to head for almost certain boat-wreck. It was by far the lesser of two evils—the alternative was some degree of crew-wreck. I checked that my life-jacket was fully inflated, and that my painting equipment and other important possessions were polythene bagged and to hand. My intention was to jump overboard with them when Epic made contact.

I pulled the tiller towards me and headed for the incisors. The stern lifted, and as Epic was rushed in on a wave, the wind then on the port quarter tried to overturn her. The few seconds taken to run the gauntlet seemed to pass in slow motion. Just a foot to starboard a large area of rock appeared to rise out of the relatively clear passage. As other sinister shapes passed inches below Epic's hull I yanked the centre-board out, cast off both sheets and bundled the mainsail/jib out of the wind, having let the halyard (the sail hoisting rope) fly. I was passing a large rocky projection to my right, prior to entering the surf and beaching, when I saw a patch of white—the bow of a boat. The flailing jib sheet I caught, passed it across the front of the mast and hauled tight on the port side. I pulled the tiller up, the jib caught the wind and Epic spun round and surged towards the gap. Without the centre-board, Epic made too much leeway. I released the jib and grabbed the oars from the gunwales, then with a few desperate strokes entered the mouth of the smallest harbour I have ever seen. A fisherman was standing by the patch of white—he had just returned from a dash through the surf to haul his nets.

"Hello." I croaked.

* At 16 feet, it was large compared to Epic.

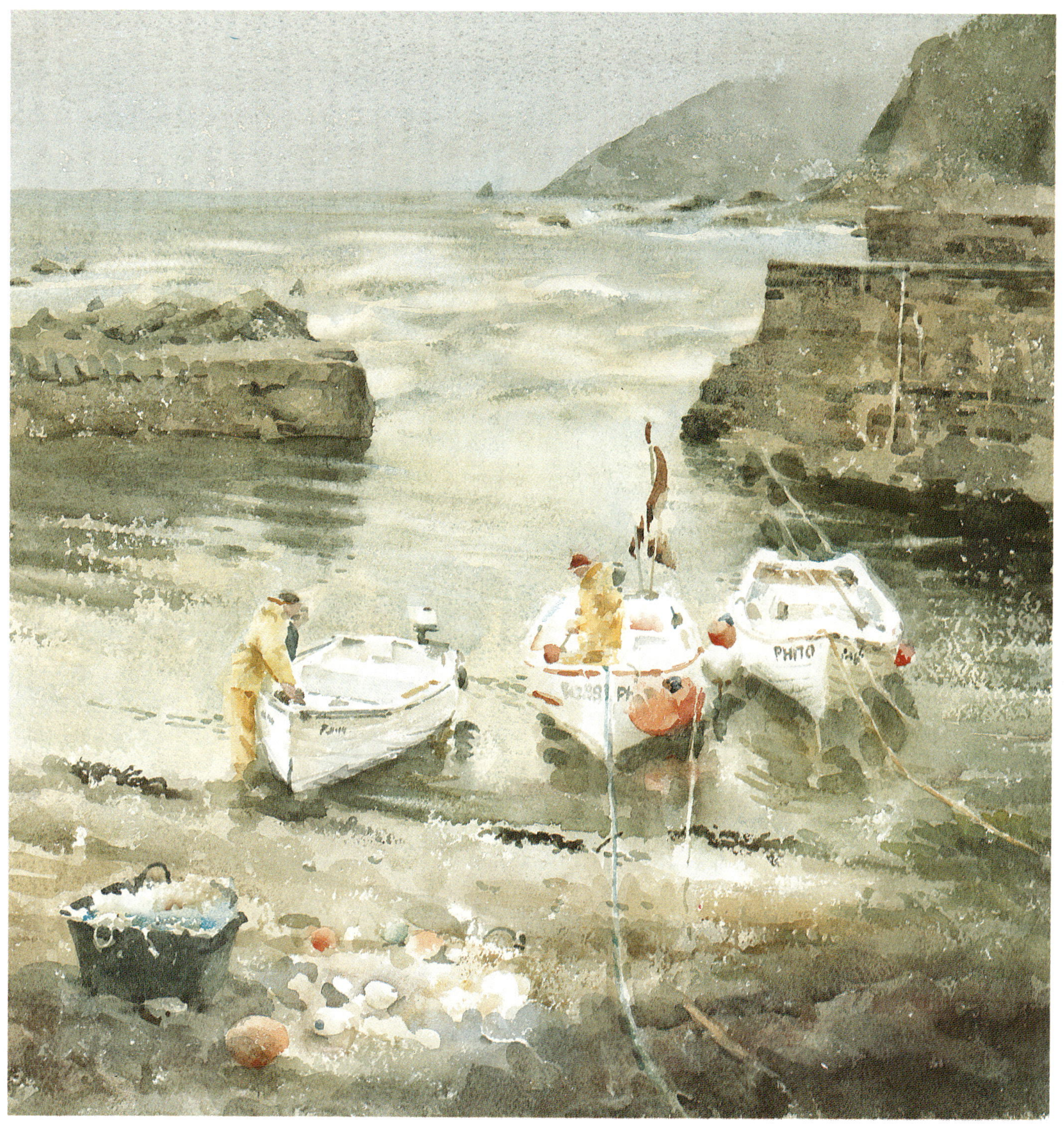

PORTWRINKLE

'"Where am I?" "Portwrinkle." He said, Matter-of-factly.'

I stepped from the dinghy a few yards inside the harbour mouth and slowly pulled Epic's bow onto the shingle. I did not feel tired but my legs felt weak. The euphoria felt after my escape caused me to take deep breaths. I wondered where I was. As my breathing and heartbeats returned to near normal, I spoke to the fisherman again.

"Where am I?"

"Portwrinkle." He said, matter-of-factly.

I had never heard of it. Cawsand is over eight miles away and Looe six miles further west, and I did not think there was a harbour between them. About five minutes later, the fisherman whose boat I had seen leaving returned with his son and some flat-fish.

"What force do you think the wind is?" I asked him.

"Six" He replied, again matter-of-factly.

An hour or so later, I de-masted and left the upturned 'miracle' above the high-water line—ready for the next part of the voyage! How soon one forgets. We were both undamaged. Again I could not believe it—but that time it was true.

Twenty hours earlier and less than two miles away I had enjoyed a pleasant sail on the Lynher River. It would have been easier to walk to Portwrinkle—but less interesting.

It was a small risk I took at the onset. When the wind increased off Long Sands I should have beached Epic while the waves were still small—at worst I would have got a little wet.

When Julia arrived two hours later to pick me up, I was chatting to a couple who had witnessed the last mile of my journey—they had expected to phone the coastguard. It really was uncanny how, at the end of an eight hour trip, I had turned at the right second and found safety.

After loading the car we looked out over the bay. Under a clear sky the sea had turned a rich turquoise blue and appeared not the least aggressive; although the wind was still strong and flecked the sea with white horses. Julia wondered what all the fuss had been about. It was high tide, and off the harbour entrance a small area of disturbed water simmered.

Flushed

I set out from Portwrinkle at 10:30am on the last day of July after strong winds had delayed my restart. Ironically, although both sails had been raised in hope, I had to row out under an overcast sky, over a smooth grey sea. A swell, resulting from the previous spell of rough weather, was noticeable where the sea lifted and fell at the base of cliffs, and there was still an area of breaking waves fifty yards off the harbour which I calmly rowed round. I lowered the white sail and pulled on the oars for a further hour, without the aid of my painting stool – it had been overlooked when unloading and was on its way back to Mevagissey. I used to wedge the stool against the foredeck – the canvas seat naturally supported my back and made rowing a delight. Two miles further on, before I reached Downderry, a faint breeze materialized from the direction of Looe – my destination, and sailing commenced. The sun came out and I sat in the bottom of the boat listening to the lap of little waves on the hull. It was idyllic – a great contrast to the end of the preceding leg. Had I not been heading just forty degrees less than straight out to sea, it would have been perfect.

At noon, my return inshore tack took me between Downderry and Seaton where I almost became becalmed. Progress towards Looe continued – row/sailing (one handed rowing to assist the sails and make a better heading). By 12:45, black sky had developed ahead and a fresh breeze blew off the land. The resulting flat sea enabled me to tack to Looe Island – which I reached at 3:30. The leaden clouds had been replaced by a brighter 'overcastness' which induced me to sail round to the lee of the shingle spit that projected towards the mainland. Day-dreams of distant uninhabited islands, and stumbling upon caches of doubloons were instantly dispelled when a cheerful middle-aged gentleman asked for the £1.50 landing fee. I was taken up to the house on the top of the island and introduced to Evelyne and Roselyn, sisters who bought the island in 1964.

After a relaxing two hour visit I slipped away to explore the river beyond Looe Bridge. High water that evening was at 9:00, which meant the one mile row round to Looe had to be undertaken post-haste in order to pass under the road bridge before the river level rose too high. (It would have been a simple matter to take the mast down). A hundred yards off the solid, circular, white topped harbour wall-end, I was passed by Erin, a converted lugger that had fished out of Mevagissey till the mid seventies. It was there one night in the late sixties that I first saw the Erin (devoid of the pleasure-boat superstructure). Her catch was being unloaded at the inner harbour jetty. The sight of the thirty eight foot, straight stemmed, rugged old boat, planked with scarred, tarred timbers, was one of my first memories after moving to Cornwall.

I entered Looe River/Harbour at half tide when the river was flowing upstream at its swiftest—6 m.p.h. In welcome sunshine, I drifted through the harbour using the oars to avoid fishing boats berthing against the east quay. Looe town can be more than a little hectic in the summer, but on the river it was relatively peaceful. The bridge seemed to offer too little headroom at first glance; then as I approached it seemed I might just make it—but would have to be quick. It was spring tides time and that day the rise was 15ft 5in (close to an inch a minute mid-tide). I shouted to a lad who was attending to warps on the boat nearest to the bridge, asking him what he thought of my chances. He gave me the palms up, shrugged shoulders answer—touch and go. Rowing quite strongly against the current I edged the mast-head an inch or two below the keystones of one of the middle arches.

Above the bridge the river divides into two. I turned to port, passed a large car-park and headed into the section not sharing its course with a railway-line. The two mile drift in sunny calm was reminiscent of my slow boat to Lerryn ride, and I hoped the outcome would be less traumatic—without deficit in my daylight and water level requirements. My exploration started in a wide mud bounded river running between wooded banks, thence to narrow, meadow-lapping stretches, and finally to the upper reaches where overhanging trees forced me to retreat. The two mile excursion turned out to be 'perfectly' uneventful.

Back down at the river junction I tied Epic against the car-park quay alongside other smallish craft which had been aground earlier. I clambered onto terra-concrete and wandered along to the Harbour Moon in West Looe to enjoy a substantial meal and quenching quart. High water was an hour away (at 9:30) which allowed me to enjoy the boating activity outside the window as I dined. As darkness fell I wandered back to my handy berth.

I moved Epic to a buoy in mid stream and was soon 'lulled' awake by the sound of car doors banging and engines revving. I wished to be on my way by 5:00 am at the latest, before the incoming tide made exiting the river difficult. Peace reigned, and I settled down for a five or six hour sleep—which I did not get.

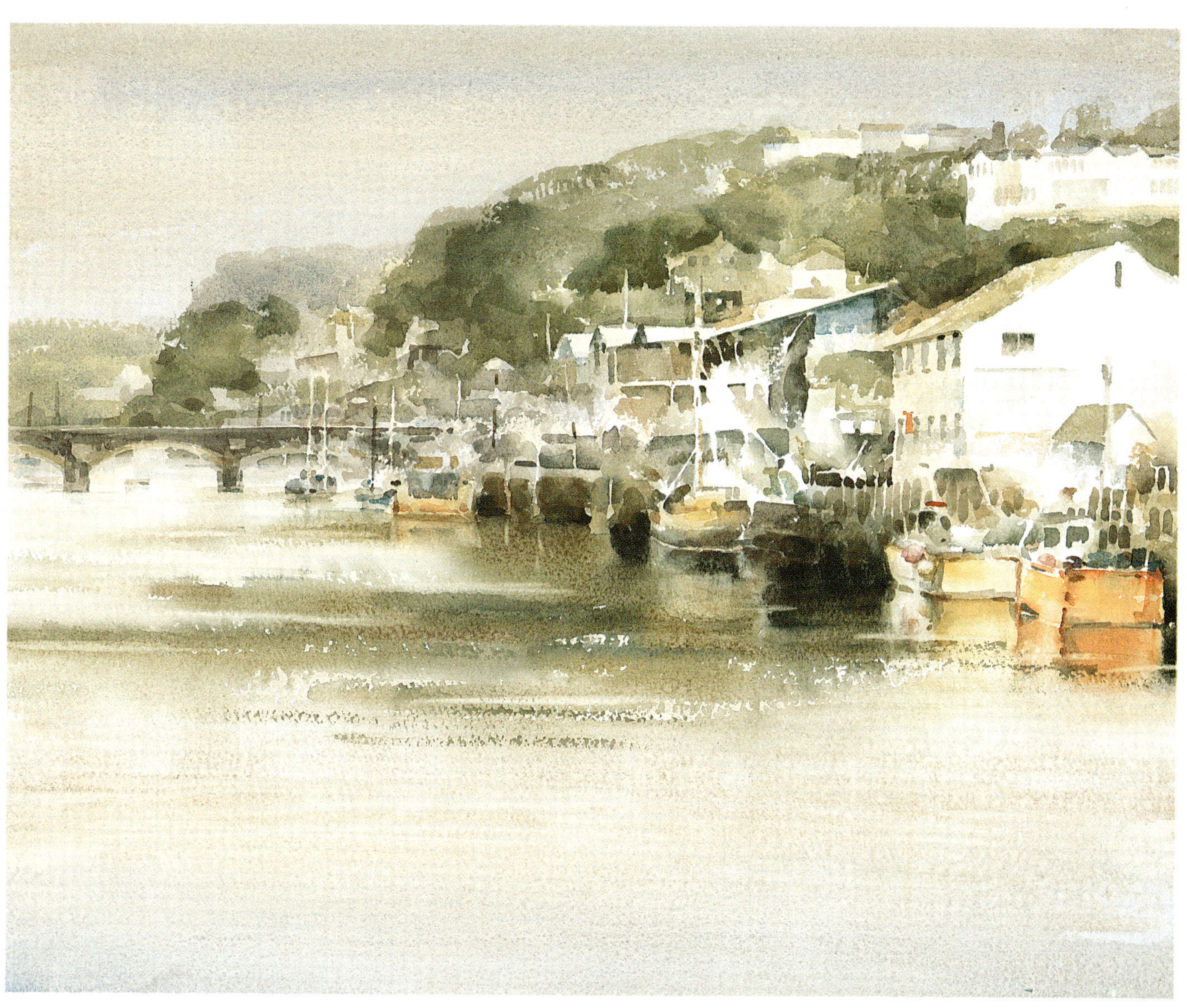

LOOE

'Rowing quite strongly against the current I edged the mast-head an inch or two below the keystones of one of the middle arches.'

August for me started before 2:00 am, for I had misjudged the depth of water and Epic started to ground. With the oars doubling as huge feelers I groped my way out of the mud maze—the lights from Looe were reflected by the water and mud alike, making it difficult to reach the main channel. Instead of finding a deep-water mooring immediately I decided to drift under the bridge. Still half asleep I was rushed down the channel unable to decide when or where to tie up. The intense darkness at the river's edge concealed all but the vague shapes of fishing boats. To one I should have tied, but I watched instead of hitching—my interrupted sleep had left me bereft of a quantity of marbles. Being on the move I thought an early start was in order and allowed myself to be swept into the night. Rational reasoning returned when I was past the harbour mouth. It was too dark to be at sea for hazards abound off Looe harbour. Besides shallows, rocks and shoals there is the Island. In sleepy stupidity, I failed to realize the significance of the remaining two or three hours of darkness.

My suicidal tendency subsided. I was unable to row upriver against the strong ebb flow so sought the floating '5 MPH' sign I had noticed in passing the evening before. I searched for it in the darkness, knowing it to be approximately a hundred yards off the river entrance. A row of amber lights fronted West Looe and cast dancing ribbon reflections across the water. After rowing against the strong tide for several minutes I noticed breaks in the ribbons which pin-pointed my emergency mooring. With great relief I passed my bow line round the sign post and wound a couple of turns about the mast—to make casting off easier.

For making an early start the speed limit sign location was most suitable but in other respects it left a lot to be desired. As I settled down to sleep, a mechanical digger man started his extremely early shift rearranging Looe Beach. Low tide in the early hours was obviously the most convenient time for beach grooming, but I could have woken unaided to hear the shipping forecast, without the growling, roaring and clanking of a caterpiller-tracked monster. A fresh and chilly offshore wind completed a night not to remember. Despite being sleeping-bagged and woolly hatted, I was extremely cold.

I have shortened my original title for this section—'Flushed From Looe' seemed a bit silly.

Rough and Smooth

'*Westerly becoming southerly, three or four, occasionally rain, good becoming moderate to poor*'. The forecast had a familiar ring, but as Polperro was under four miles away and I expected a favourable beam wind for the first two miles, I left immediately. I slipped away from the signpost, set both sails and sped over the relatively flat sea heading for the channel between the mainland and the island. The power created by the two small sails amazed me, but before I could settle down to enjoy the performance, the wind died. The cold rush, out of the Looe River, was having its last laugh. Taking the rough with the smooth is fair enough – but the smooth was also a bit rough, for I had to row.

Rowing became second nature. (The first – waiting for the rain to cease). On a syrupy sea, I left behind duplicate rows of concentric circles that became fainter as they continued to radiate, finally coalescing with the misty dawn. The sun broke through the cloud cover ten degrees above Looe Island and within a few minutes blue sky predominated. Just before reaching the first headland, guarded by the Hore Stone (a large rocky outcrop similar to the Long Stone), I observed the first sign of the returning wind. 'Cat's-paws' (groups of delicate mini-waves a few inches apart) ruffled the surface and were soon replaced by proper little waves. I reverted to sail-power and tacked out to sea. Mist had shrouded the higher ground when my return tack took me into Talland Bay. The same prevailed at the end of the next tack as I rounded Downend Point and sighted Polperro. With a freshening wind heading me I rowed the last half mile to the harbour under a clearing sky, and in bright sunshine entered possibly the most picturesque harbour in Cornwall.

In the stern of a fishing boat stood the archetypal Cornish fisherman. I rowed over and asked the navy-jumpered, denim-jeaned, stocky, weather-beaten faced seaman, if he could suggest a spot where Epic could safely lie for an hour or so. The kind gentleman advised me to tie up against a row of 'giant ladders' just inside the harbour mouth on the right. I stepped ashore and strolled through the narrow walk-ways round to the other side of the harbour and looked across at my diminutive dinghy. What she lacked in size was compensated for by the purposeful way she sat on the water, her flat nose pointing seaward catching the morning sun. Tidily stowed on the gunwales were the oars. The red jib was neatly bundled at the base of the forestay and the white sail was carefully wrapped around the mast. She looked ship-shape and set for adventure. I felt proud of Epic.

Sitting outside a cafe, I drank a mug of tea while appreciating the haphazard beauty of the cottages that had evolved on the steep harbour-side. The little stone bridge at the entrance of the harbour (like the one at Lerryn) was a simple, satisfying structure – pure functional engineering. The banishment of most motor cars had been an important factor in my enjoyment of the shore sortie to Polperro. Before I left, a helpful sun-bather, at my request, supplied me with a measure of lotion to protect my face from the reflected glare of the rare rays. At 10:30, under a powerful sun, I resumed my journey into the wind, hoping sun-tan oil would play a more prominent role, and August would continue its seasonal ways.

After row/sailing a little over a mile to Larrick, with the wind on the port bow, I downed sail and rowed into the wind a further mile and a half which put me a mile off West Coombe. I resumed sailing and hoped to pass Pencarro Head and reach Lantic Bay, but the wind strengthened and a choppy sea forced me well short of my target. Before rounding the headland I had to make four tacks. When completing the first, close to the cliffs, the linen hat I thought wedged firmly on my head blew off. With a fresh wind and lumpy sea to contend with it was quite awkward coming about in an attempt to retrieve it. Although my lunging boat-hook made contact I failed to catch the hat and did not get a second chance – for it sank surprisingly quickly. As the distorted disc faded, so to some extent did my spirits – the hat was of sentimental value. (I acquired it at Ephesus during my Turkey trip the previous June. It helped make possible the production of three watercolours on the day of purchase when the temperature reached 40°C). During the last two tacks, to counteract the landward drift, I assisted with the port-side oar while working the tiller with my left hand.

I was frightened in the period shortly after losing my hat. By 3:30 I was getting tired – it was necessary to use both oars to gain sea-room. When Washing Rocks, the point where I could bear away and enter the River Fowey, was two miles away, my progress was barely on the right side of stationary. I should have returned to Polperro, but the thought did not occur to me. Fear and tiredness had once more overruled my ability to assess the situation and take appropriate action. Although twice the distance, a return trip to Polperro would have been quicker and infinitely safer than battling on to Fowey.

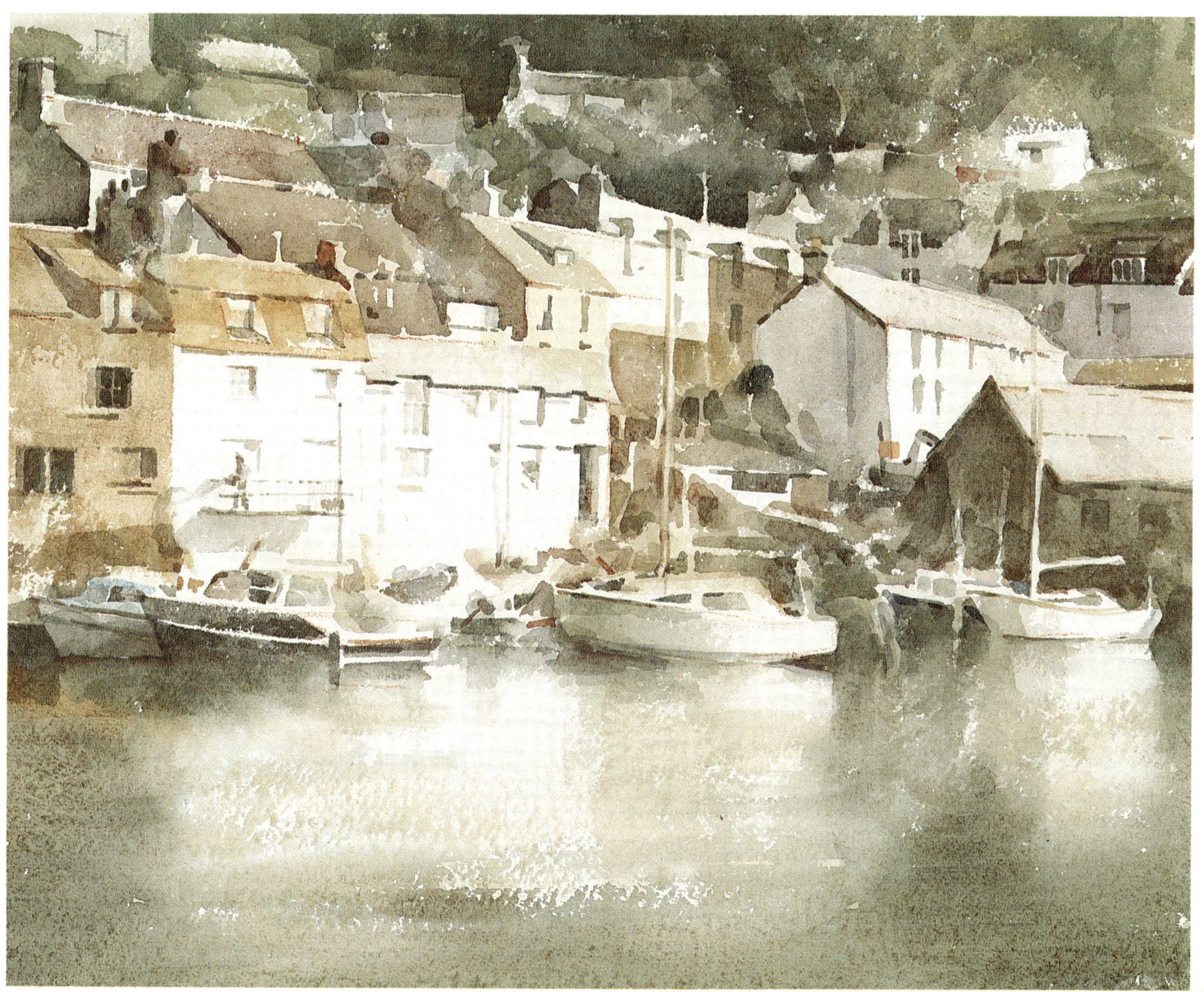

POLPERRO

'With a freshening wind heading me I rowed the last half mile to the harbour under a clearing sky, and in bright sunshine entered possibly the most picturesque harbour in Cornwall.'

On reaching Lantic Bay I saw the crew and passengers of half a dozen various craft preparing to return to Fowey or Polruan. The increased wind strength had cut short their afternoon on the beach, and their proximity reduced my anxiety. Twice, as I struggled on for a further hour, I was asked if I needed a tow. One offer came from a duo in a dinghy, similar in length to Epic and propelled by a tiny buzzing outboard motor. It progressed slightly quicker, and danced precariously over the waves.

The wind moderated, and with renewed spirits I enjoyed the half mile row to the entrance of the Fowey River. It was an exciting ride over a very confused sea—without regimentation from the wind, irregular waves were formed. I passed between St Catherine's Castle and the smaller fortification on Punches Cross Rocks, on the Polruan (east) side, and reached calm water.

Fowey Harbour and the last mile of the river are one, making it an interesting area to explore. On the sheltered stretch of water, ocean going ships pass a few yards in front of steep wooded banks, and may be replaced within seconds by swans, canoes, or a little sailing dinghy. Passenger ferries cross the river in front of large solid tug-boats moored mid-channel, and between yachts of all sizes heading out or returning from the open sea. Pont Pill creek contains dozens of moorings in a most heavenly setting. It meanders from a narrow stream to form a mile long tributary which is three hundred yards wide where it joins the main river opposite Fowey. After threading my way between moored boats off Polruan—a relatively quiet backwater, I crossed the river, and aided by the sedate beginning of the flood tide I made my way leisurely along the Fowey fore-shore. A great variety of dwellings stand on the river's rocky edge. Many have overhanging verandas or balconies, or both; and some have ladders, from which at most states of the tide, escape from the motor congested narrow street is possible.

The sun was shining when I returned to Caffa Mill late in the afternoon. Six weeks previously an unnamed little blue boat had proved eminently suitable at river drifting. As Epic, she had graduated to survive sea shakeups, and given me a greater respect for the sea—particularly when it caresses in boisterous mood the rocky cliffs of Cornwall. Sporting a pay and display sticker, Epic did not look too out of place between the white lines in the car-park where I left her overnight. I hoped the wind the following day would be abeam—or in non-nautical terms, on our side.

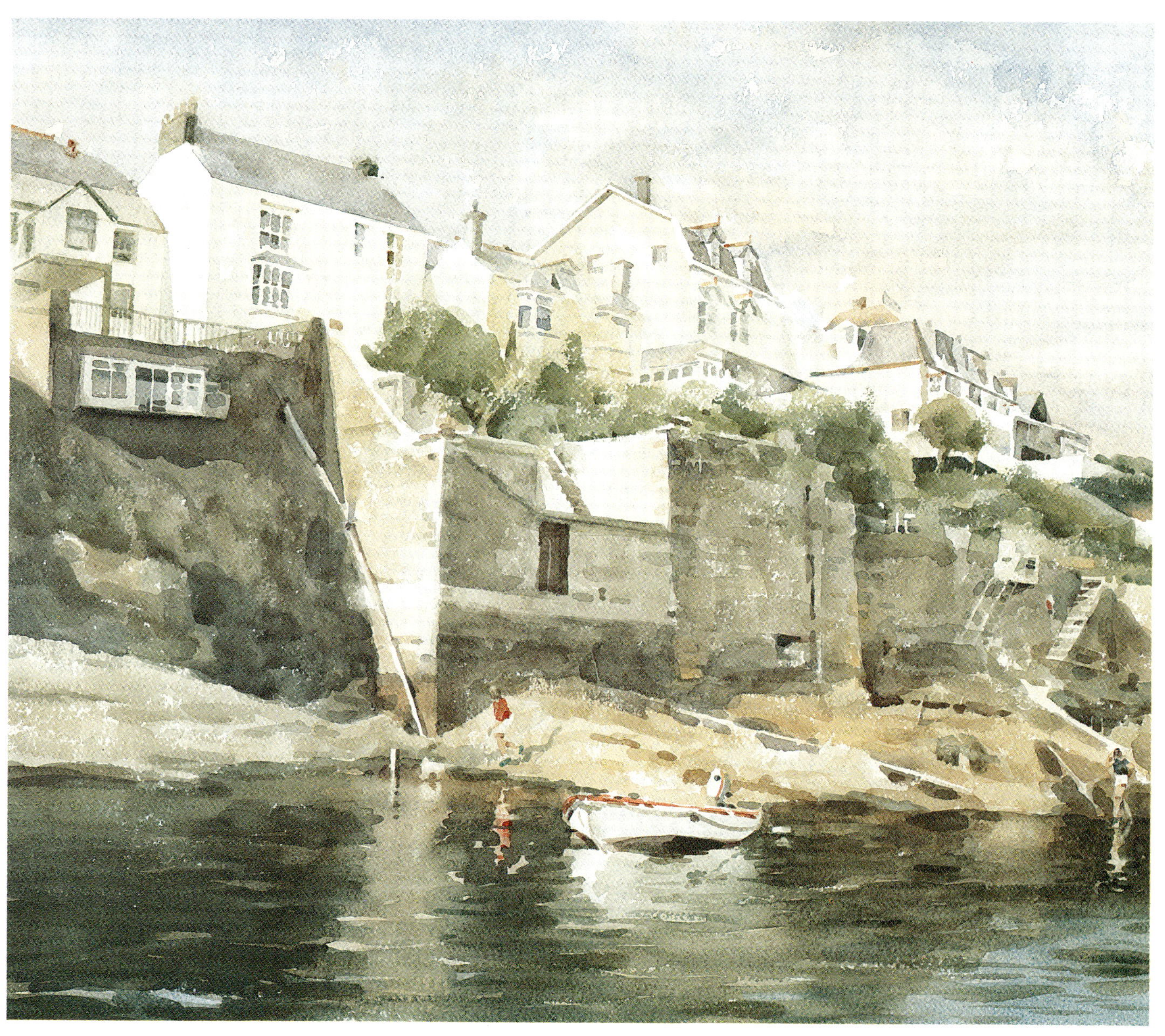

FOWEY

'Aided by the sedate beginning of the flood tide I made my way leisurely along the Fowey fore-shore.'

Edward, my youngest son, took me for a row on the river before I left Fowey the next morning. It was exactly high tide which prevented us drifting far from the slip. The car ferry docked close by so I thought it prudent to assist the eight year old to vacate the immediate area, and allow him to concentrate on his ins and outs away from the ferry's path.

Sailing in the lee of Fowey I made my way to the sea. Though agitated the river was flat up to the fortifications and just a couple of tacks were needed before I entered the swells off the craggy coastline leading to Gribbin Head. In warm sunshine the sailing was enjoyable and I was comfortable in shirt and jeans. Polridmouth, a cove cradled by cliffs and overlooked from Menabilly, was relatively calm and looked most inviting, but I was a month behind schedule and sailed by. There were to be many other locations that delays, caused by the worst June/July weather in Cornwall for many years, forced me to leave unexplored.

By one o'clock, after a tough hour of row/sailing and tacking, I reached a point between the Gribbin (headland) and Cannis Rock – a mile and a half out from the harbour entrance. Cannis Rock is covered at high-water but still leaves a large area of confused sea even in moderate winds. I entered the area of unpredictable waves as I moved out of the headland's protection and found progress in the confused, wind-blown sea a little slow. I thought twice about continuing, and reasoned that further into St Austell Bay the motion should be easier, and if not I could run back to Fowey. Later I could retreat down the other side of the headland, past Little Gribbin towards Polkerris or Par. Donning my life-jacket, I carried on. (By that time I should have been wearing it, but it is easy to forget important safety measures when starting out in mild conditions). As I was thinking of putting on my waterproof jacket, a dollop of rogue wave top soaked me. I left the jacket off to allow the sun and wind to dry my shirt. In the few minutes taken to squeeze the few pints of sea-water overboard I was frozen, and it was bliss to don the oilskin – although wet I was warm. I had received a practical lesson regarding the dangerous wind-chill factor – fortunately in ideal conditions. Grey skies returned and remained for the rest of the day.

I had planned to follow the coastline round St Austell Bay and call in at Charlestown – a small harbour capable of being squeezed into by ships of up to eight thousand tons which are 'locked' in while taking on board cargoes of china clay. From the Gribbin, the best course I could make was towards Chapel Point, passing three miles off Charlestown and missing Mevagissey by a mile – which I thought quite satisfactory. I would then be able to wend my way home in the shelter of familiar coastline. Anxiously I set out to cross St Austell and Mevagissey Bays, and sailing about seventy five degrees off the wind I made good progress. The rigging looked so frail and the thin ply still seemed hardly sufficient protection against the endless succession of little waves that Epic pounded through.

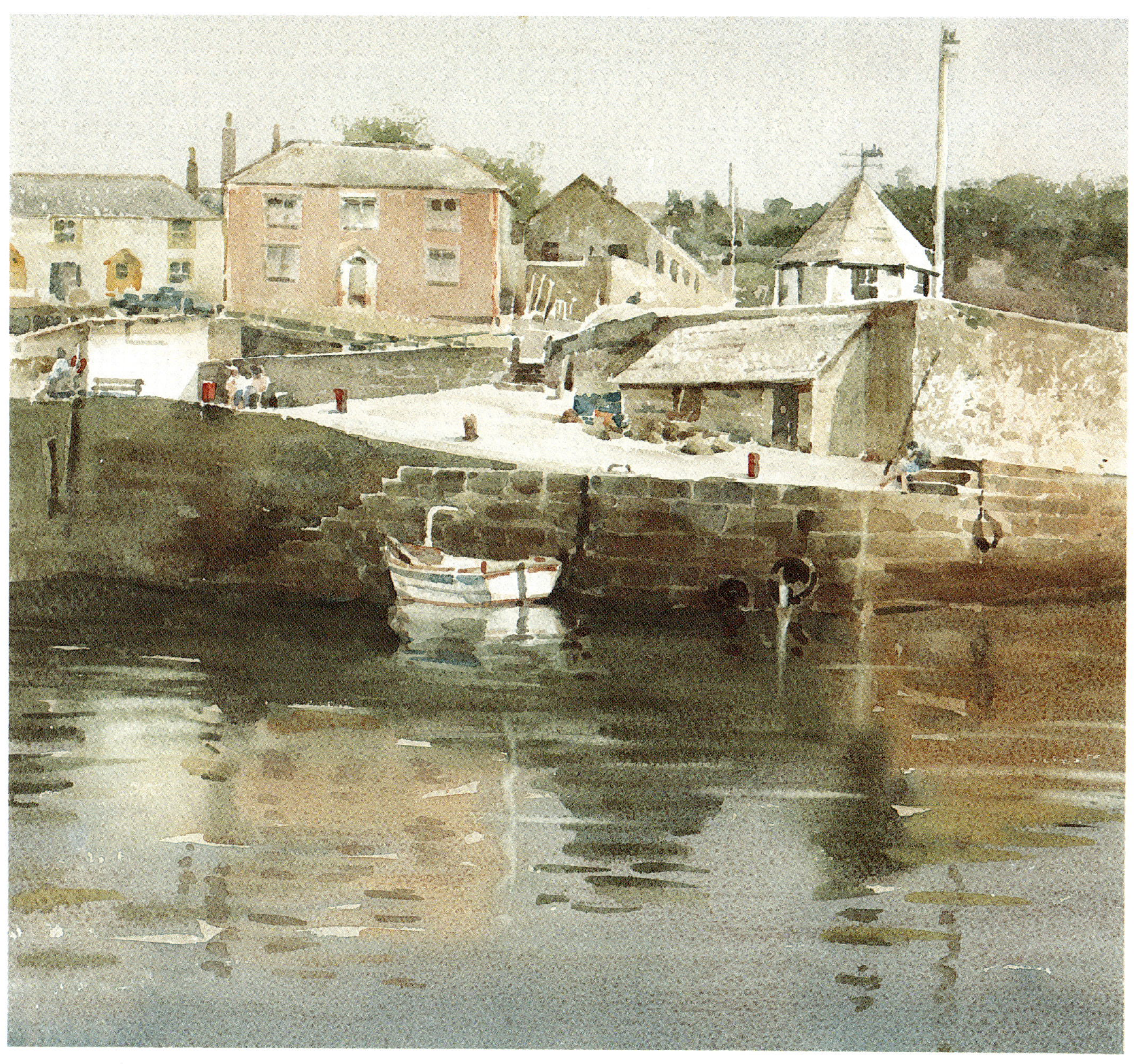

CHARLESTOWN

The earth's curvature was apparent when I looked back to Par from half-way across the Bays. From my low vantage point a section of watery sphere obscured the foreshore and the lower part of the chimneys of the china clay drying plant. Noticing the phenomena when so close to land made the world appear very small. Had I been able to head down the Channel and sail on round the world at that speed (3 mph ish) I would have returned in about a year—perhaps not so small.

After an hour or so I became accustomed to Epic's vigorous motion and tried to take a photograph while steering with my feet. Bucking Epic and I nearly parted company, so I held on to the boat and snapped single-handed.

When a mile from Chapel Point I looked towards peaceful Pentewan which lay two miles abeam and recalled happy times. For three years in the early seventies Julia and I lived and ran a gallery there. The faint pale line of sandy beach which lies to the west of the village was visible. From there, aided by fellow shopkeeper John, I launched a fourteen foot clinker sailing dinghy. Though two decades have passed, I can still remember the embarrassment I felt at our amateur performance. We wheeled the heavy boat round the old dock and down to the water's edge. Then having rolled our jeans knee-high we pushed the dinghy into the sea. A minute later I was grimly hanging on to the bow, having been lifted off the sea-bed by waves that passed over my head.

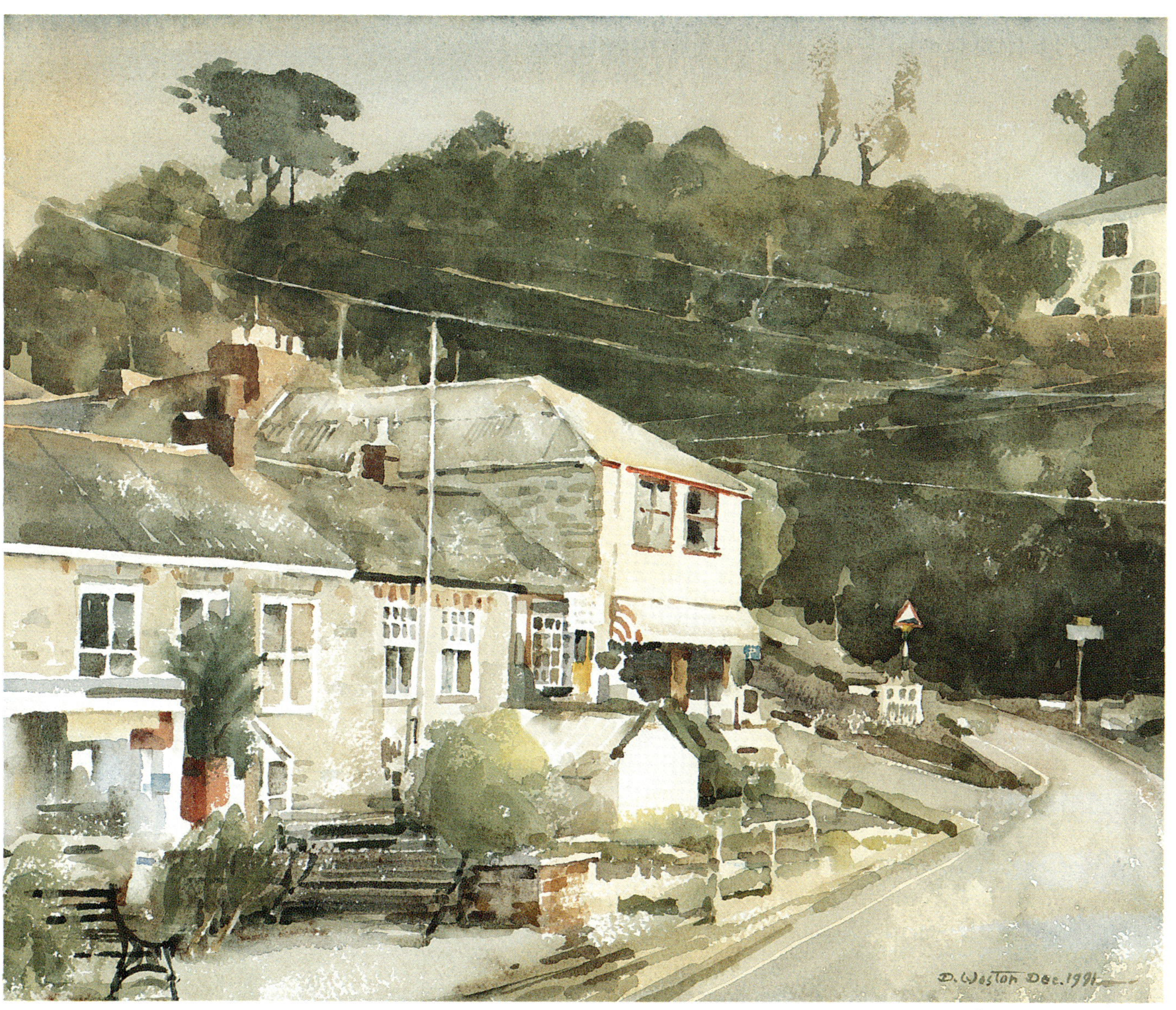

PENTEWAN

'– I looked towards peaceful Pentewan which lay two miles abeam and recalled happy times.'
(The building with the sun-blind was our home and gallery)

The wind kept up well till I joined a few pleasure and angling boats in the lee of Chapel Point. With a feeling of relief at being in home waters I followed the rocky peninsular round to the cove at Portmellon where a heavily constructed steel slipway runs down to a sandy beach. Alas, few new boats now enter the sea from the slip—the old sheds of Mitchell's Boatyard have given way to development. Before it became history, I painted several watercolours in the dingy atmospheric splendour of the chaotic interior. The cove, with its gently shelving sandy beach, has the added attraction of a handy inn—The Rising Sun. A dozen or so holidaymakers were enjoying their last few minutes on the beach. It began drizzling before I reached Mevagissey—a quarter of a mile away.

I downed sail and rowed into the outer harbour past the lighthouse at the end of the East Quay. After passing between visiting yachts at anchor, I tied up temporarily alongside the middle steps on the other side. Charlie, who had been hoping for customers to take a trip with him round the bay, called it a day and motored off to his outer harbour mooring. The drizzle turned to rain and I wandered off with my lidded plastic buckets to check out the gallery. Later that evening, towards high water, I bailed out Epic and rowed to the slip in the inner harbour where the boys were waiting to lift Epic on to the trolley. I then pushed my little voyager home, round the one way system, and parked her on the front lawn behind a clump of marguerites.

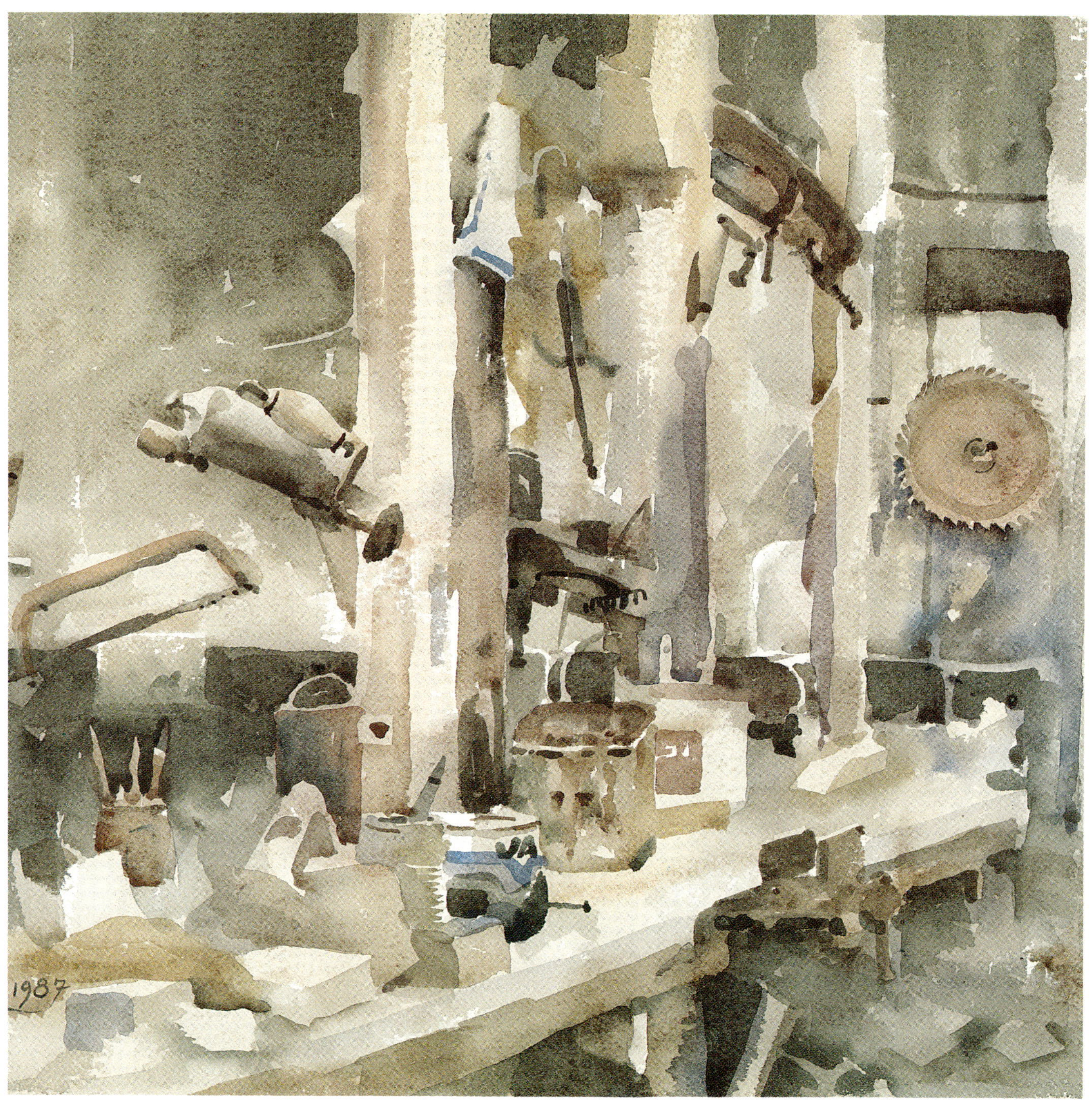

OLD BOAT-SHED, Portmellon

'Before it became history, I painted several watercolours in the dingy atmospheric splendour of the chaotic interior.'

Sleeping Ogre

I spent a few days in my gallery while waiting for settled weather in which to round the dreaded headland, Dodman (Deadman) Point which lay four miles to the south. I had been away longer than intended, and seeing empty spaces between the paintings caused me to wince somewhat. The trip could have been completed the next summer, but my heart was set on completing the voyage—sailing into Carrick Roads and on to Truro.

During the following few days I rendered a minor spot of rot on the bow into a major white blemish on the varnish—my liberal use of filler and paint being far from cosmetic. Some of the slight abrasions, received by Epic when left 'grazing' alongside the outer-harbour steps, I also treated.

On August 8th a force four north-west wind was forecast—the maximum Epic could manage with safety would be coming off the land, and a flattish sea could be expected close inshore. Smoother water meant speedier progress and a better heading into the wind. I aimed to be off the Dodman around 11:00 am (slack low water) but had to leave the inner harbour slip three hours before—while there was still sufficient water to launch.

After stowing the gear and raising the mast while still in the front garden (Epic's mast easily passed under the overhead cables en-route to the harbour), I guided the trolley carrying my transport/accommodation unit down to the slipway. Ten minutes later, having placed the trolley in the gallery (an incongruous exhibit), I was rowing out of the inner harbour.

A faint following wind filled the red jib as I ghosted out past Portmellon and on towards Chapel Point. I did not set the half bikini top, for I had time on my hands, but hoped the semisphere would be stretched in action later in the day to help Epic breast the waves to Carrick Roads. In warm sunshine under a blue sky I enjoyed a most delightful sail—reminiscent of the dolphin encounter period to which I was treated after passing Rame head. There was just sufficient wind to make headway, and I rounded the peninsular on which stands a mini-hamlet in private spendour. The three dwellings (1934-39) were planned and built by the architect John Campbell with the help of a skilled mason and carpenter. He set out to show that quality work, using traditional methods and materials, was a viable alternative to constructions that were being produced using ever more skimpy, manufactured components. Many more fine houses were designed to occupy the impressive site, but sadly the artistry of the accomplished architect was ended—when walking home one foggy night, after a visit to a Mevagissey pub, he fell to his death from the cliff-top.

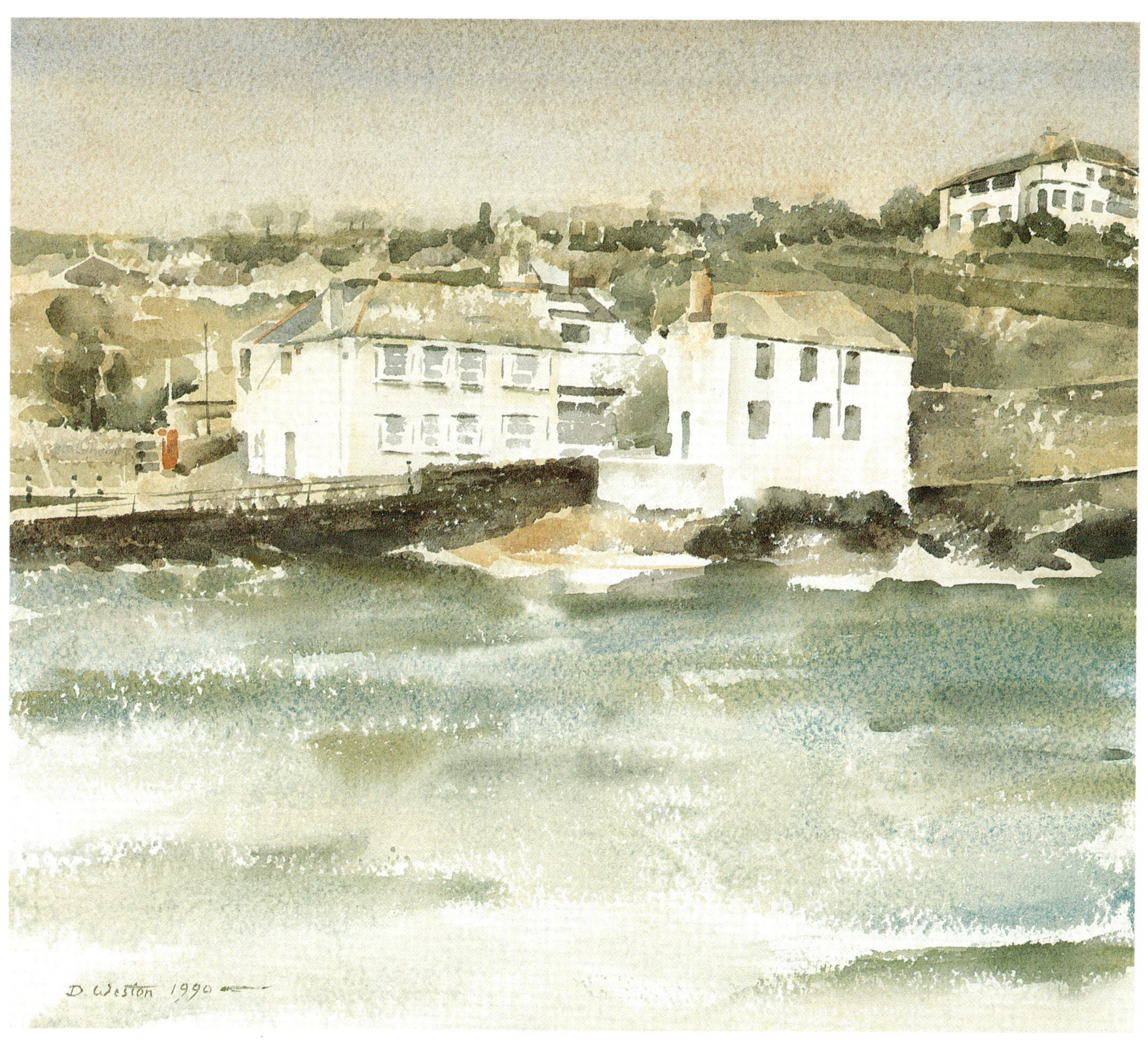

PORTMELLON

'With a feeling of relief at being in home waters I followed the rocky peninsular round to the cove at Portmellon, – .'

A herd of 'holidaying' cows often frequent the otherwise peaceful location of Colona Beach—tucked in tightly on the west side of Chapel Point. Two miles on, I ran Epic gently into the sandy beach a few yards along from Gorran Haven's sturdy stone harbour wall. Inside the protective arm about twenty boats lay listing, or legged (supported by outboard uprights), waiting for the tide to turn. At that relatively early hour many folk were enjoying the rare luxury of perfect beach weather. Occasional token waves were flipping and swishing up to Epic's sun-warmed stern as I wandered up the steep narrow hill between tightly packed old stone cottages. On the seaward side, a towered church has somehow been squeezed into the story-book village.

I called to see Stuart, who was putting a finishing touch to a cottage with sea views that he had built. I hoped to collect the white jib which I had returned to him a few days earlier when friends of his wished to use his dinghy. 'Unfortunately', the weather being idyllic, the friends had planned to sail again that day. (I am sure he would have lent me the sail had he known my deficiency). Optimistically, I imagined myself spinnakering all the way to St Anthony Head. Returning to the beach with Stuart we met the 'guard Don', sitting protectively by the open doors of the boathouse. Within the gloom still lay the little gem that I had cast an envious eye over three months earlier. Looking down the beach at Epic, set against a sparkling backdrop of sun spangled sea, I felt no desire to swap—but I could have made use of a triangular piece of tan coloured canvas. The direction I wished to sail from the Dodman was more or less the same as that from Chapel Point to Gorran Haven. As the red jib had performed admirably and stronger winds were expected, I felt happy to take part in a 100% reduction sail.

At 10:10 I continued my carefree cruise, and within the hour I was passing within a few yards of the sunlit craggy cliffs of the Dodman and was amazed at the tranquillity. Almost becalmed and steering with my feet I could have glided over and patted the 'infamous ogre'.

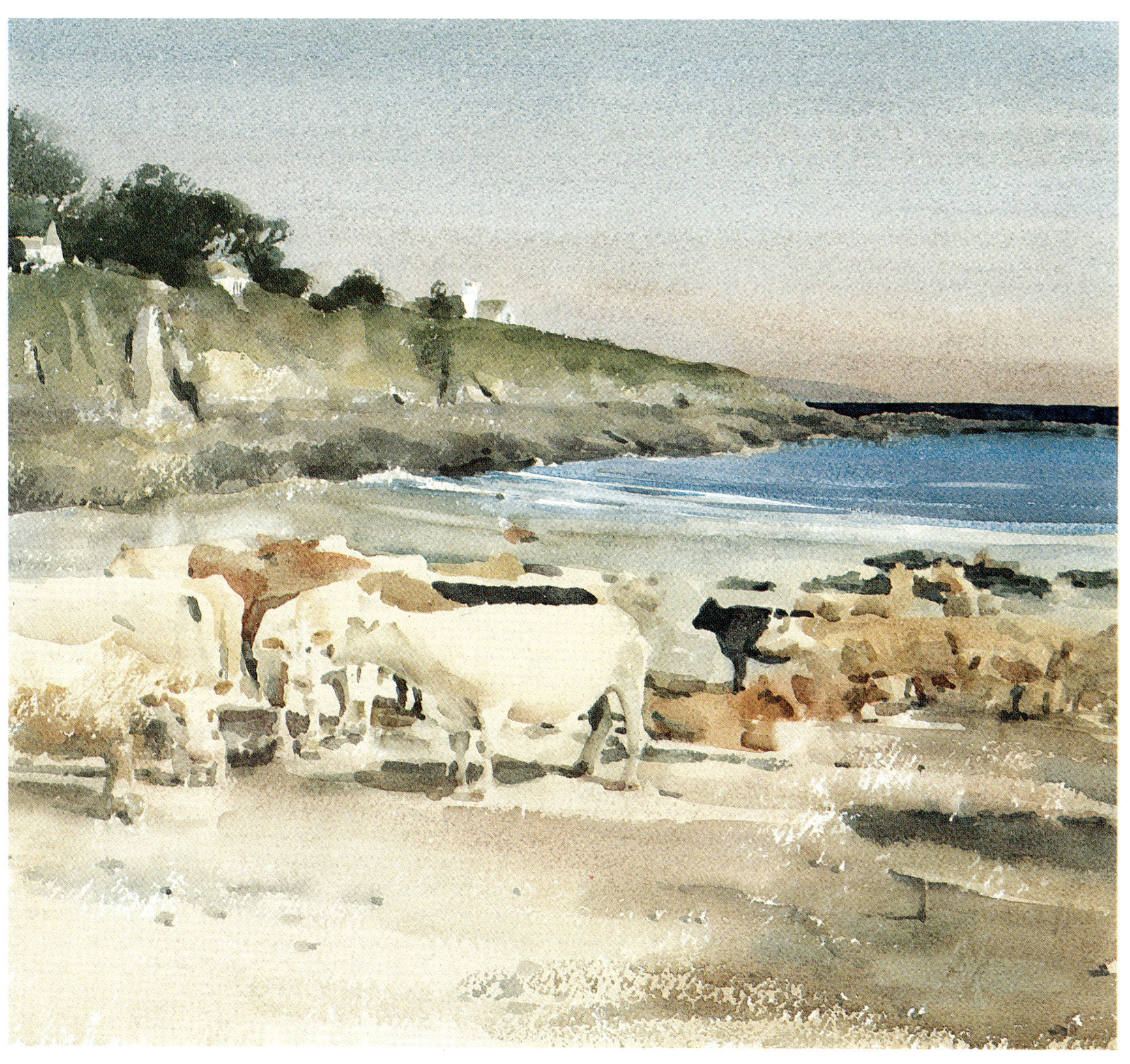

COLONA BEACH, Chapel Point

'A herd of 'holidaying' cows often frequent the otherwise peaceful location of Colona Beach.'

Long Haul

The realization, that under jib alone I would miss Zone Point and be carried way out to sea, came to me half an hour after leaving the protection of the Dodman. To have tacked inland towards Hemmick Beach—just to the west of the Dodman, would have all but halted progress. The rugged cliffs were interrupted by the pleasant sandy beaches of Hemmick and Porthluney Cove (where I had planned to stop and paint Caerhays Castle). The wind direction was fine for visiting the Veryan Bay Locations, but there was no time. Peaceful Portholland and Portloe were also regrettably left in my wake.

The wind was too westerly and I had to assist the small unbalanced sail with oar-power. I hoped for a favourable wind-shift and settled down to the task of completing the long haul. It was most frustrating battling against the elements in what were perfect sailing conditions for a properly rigged boat. I encountered yachts heading east, being wafted along effortlessly, and wished for a few hours of down wind sailing. The steep sided Gull Rock that rises from the sea half a mile from the coast, east of Nare Head, was a progress marker that took hours to edge along the coastline to Portloe. By 4:00, Portscatho at the west end of Gerrans Bay lay about two miles north-west. I had covered approximately two thirds of the distance towards Zone Point from the Dodman (they are eleven miles apart) and not surprisingly I was shattered.

A dozen or so sailing cruisers passed close to me during the crossing and thoughtful skippers from three or four checked to see how I was faring. One fine gaff cutter, possibly heading to Fowey, passed a few hundred yards to starboard; then a minute or so later sped back close hauled, pressed over ten degrees by the vast taut mainsail and full foresail that stretched from sprit-end to masthead. She came about, and as the helmsman eased her twenty eight feet, plus ten of bow-sprit slowly by, he asked if I needed help. Little Epic, two to three miles offshore, with the scrap of sail hoisted on her stumpy mast and an automaton flailing away with a pair of oars, certainly looked in need of help (or some kind of certification). I felt privileged to have witnessed at close quarters the performance of the symphony in white. (The hull, sails and the simple cabin top were white). The spars, gunwales, rubbing-strake and grab-rails were of varnished timber which delicately trimmed the aptly named 'Temptress'. I thanked the considerate seaman for his thoughtfulness.

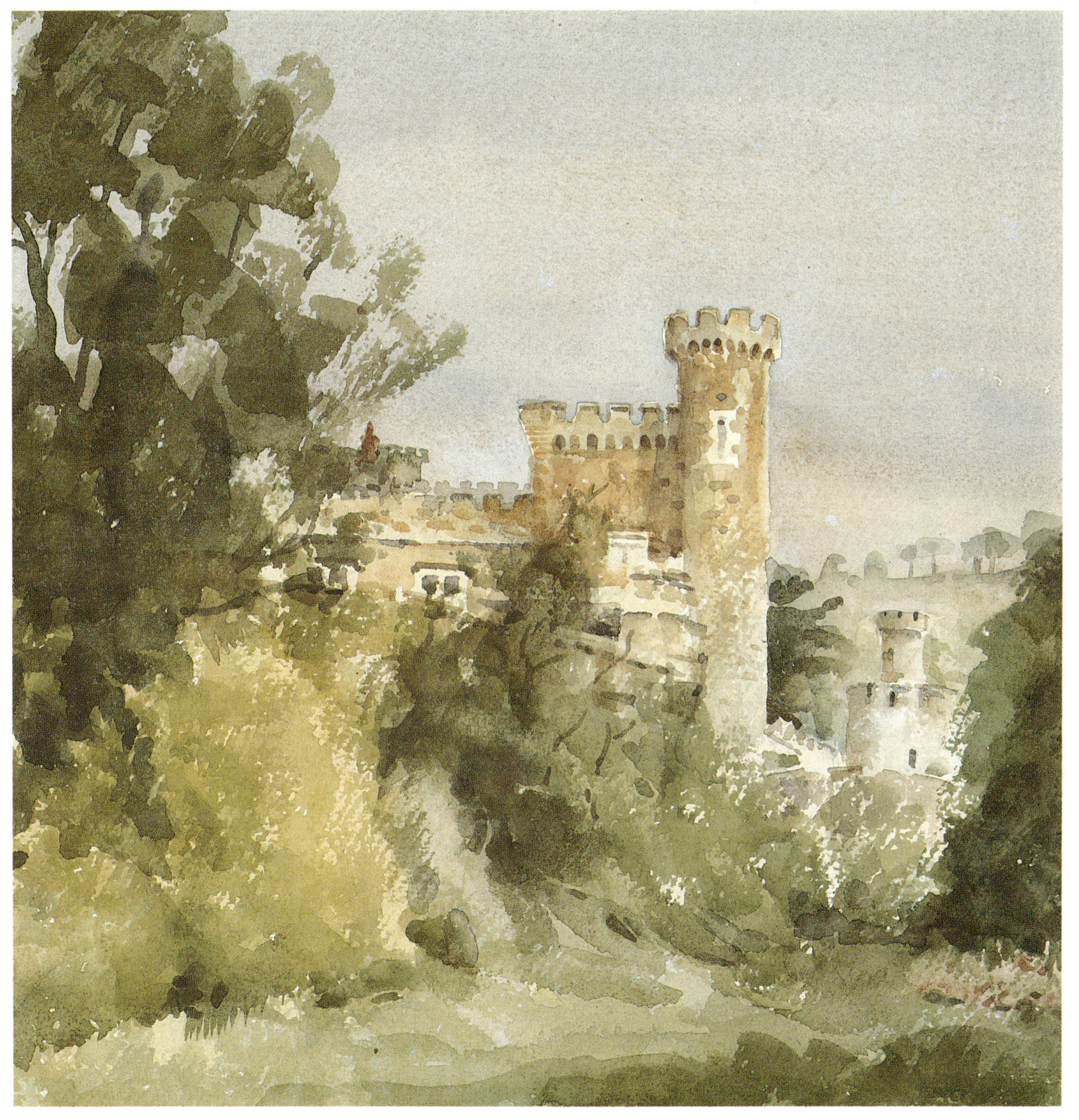

CAERHAYS CASTLE

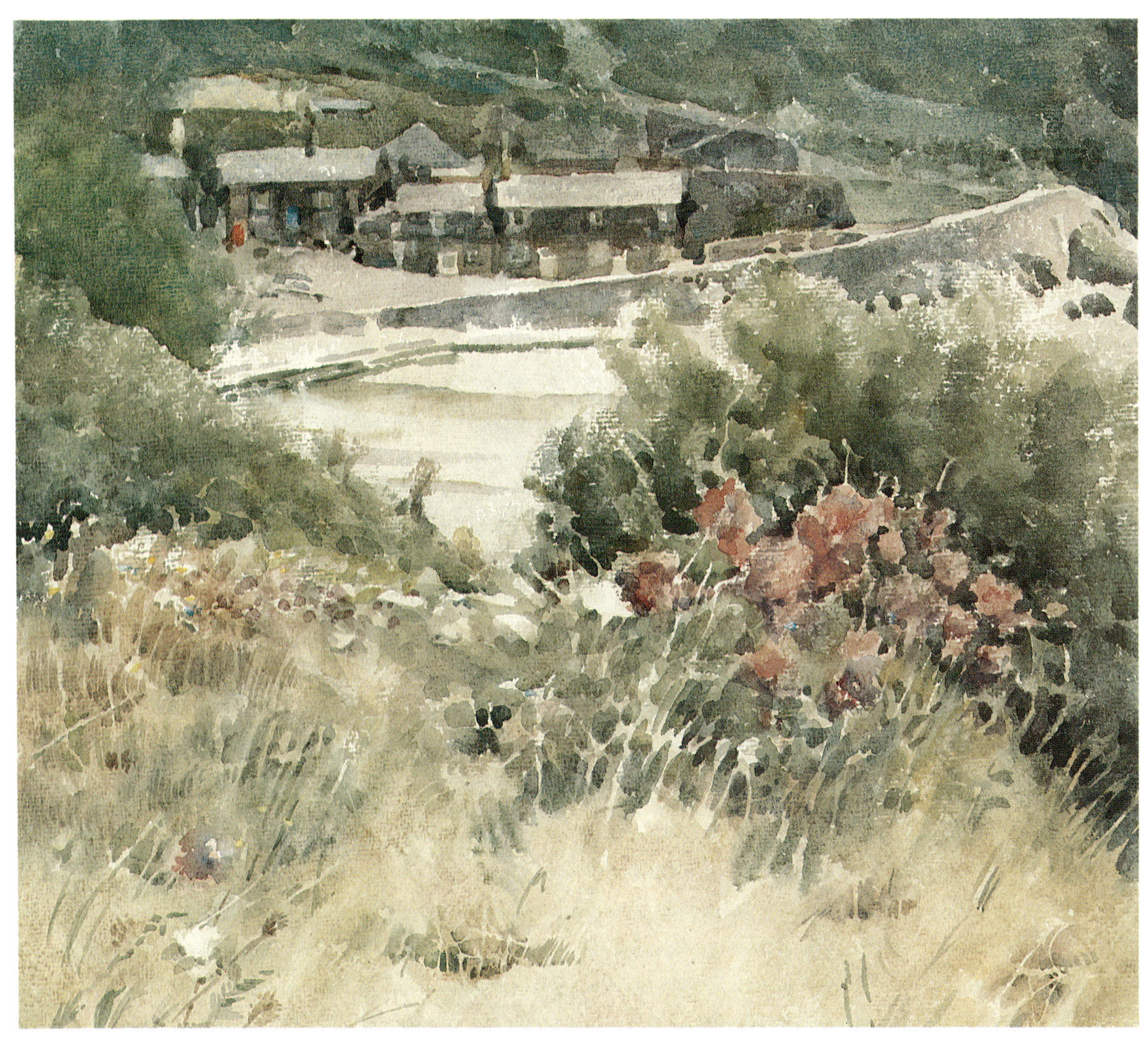

PORTHOLLAND

'Peaceful Portholland and Portloe were also, regrettably, left in my wake.'

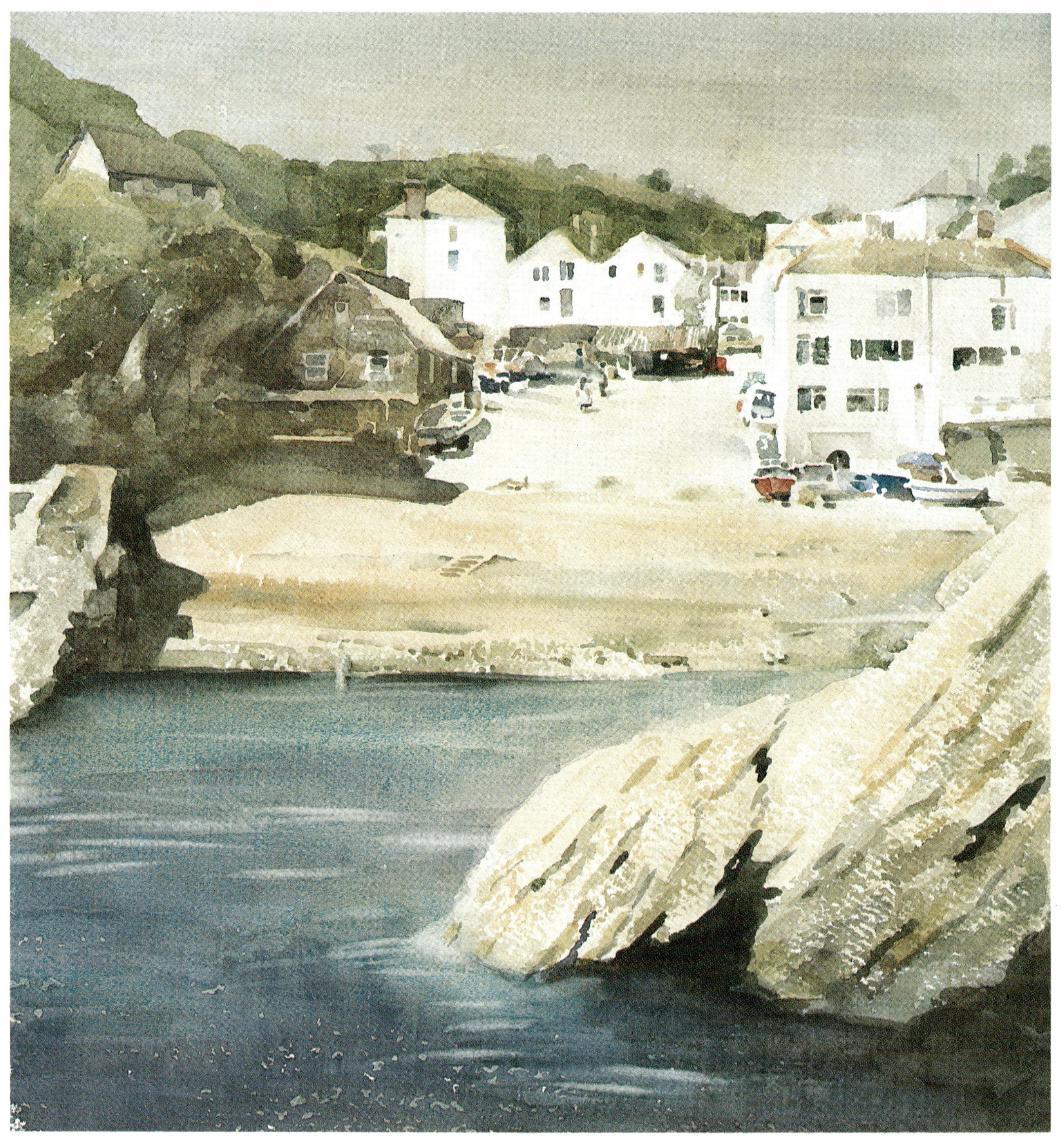

PORTLOE

By 6:00 I thought I was bidding a thankful farewell to the open sea. I was close in off Zone Point with St Anthony Head, the eastern sentinel of Carrick Roads, a mere six hundred yards away. I tried to head towards Pendennis Castle—which stands guard opposite St Anthony Head, but the wind funnelled out of the mile wide channel raising uncomfortable waves that forced Epic further out to sea. Several offers of a tow to calmer waters were made during the hour or so that I thrashed and tacked between the headlands. Had I accepted assistance, when only a mile from port, my hastened supping would have been tinged with regret—I hoped to salute the defeated, decidedly non-seasonal Neptune, at the conclusion of a solo encounter.

It was after 7:00 when I tangled with rocks at the foot of St Anthony Light after slowly fighting my way across the wakes of the returning armada—the pleasure craft being taken back to moorings in the creeks, harbours and marinas that are legion in the region. By the time I entered the mouth of Percuil River and bore away to St Mawes the wind had moderated and the sea calmed down considerably. Above the castle, for magical moments, a show of 'fiery diffused stained glass' sparkled as multicoloured spinnakers 'floated' across the evening sun.

With great relief I pulled down the red jib, and in the gathering gloom rowed to the slip where I tethered Epic. For virtually the whole of the previous ten hours I had been rowing and so it was, with hands set in glass-holding mode, I made my way up to the Victory Inn—less than fifty yards away. My liquid salutation was interrupted from time to time by my popping down to Epic to re-float her. The shelving shingle harbour-bottom drained rapidly, and when my lengthy bow line no longer reached the slip I tied Epic to a more than adequate lump of rock which I manhandled down the beach periodically.

Rejuvenated, I promenaded to a nearby take-away, purchased chicken and chips and devoured the overdue sustenance while standing beside Epic in the gloom. One is likely to raise cuisine ratings when hungry—I would have given the wrapping several stars. Having completed the strenuous leg (and chips) I felt elated, and was happy to row across the still water to an 'Edam' off St Anthony. I slipped into my sleeping bag, and in the comforting privacy of darkness reflected on the day's events. I savoured a second supper of Mars bars and orange-juice, then drifted arm-achingly, but happily to sleep.

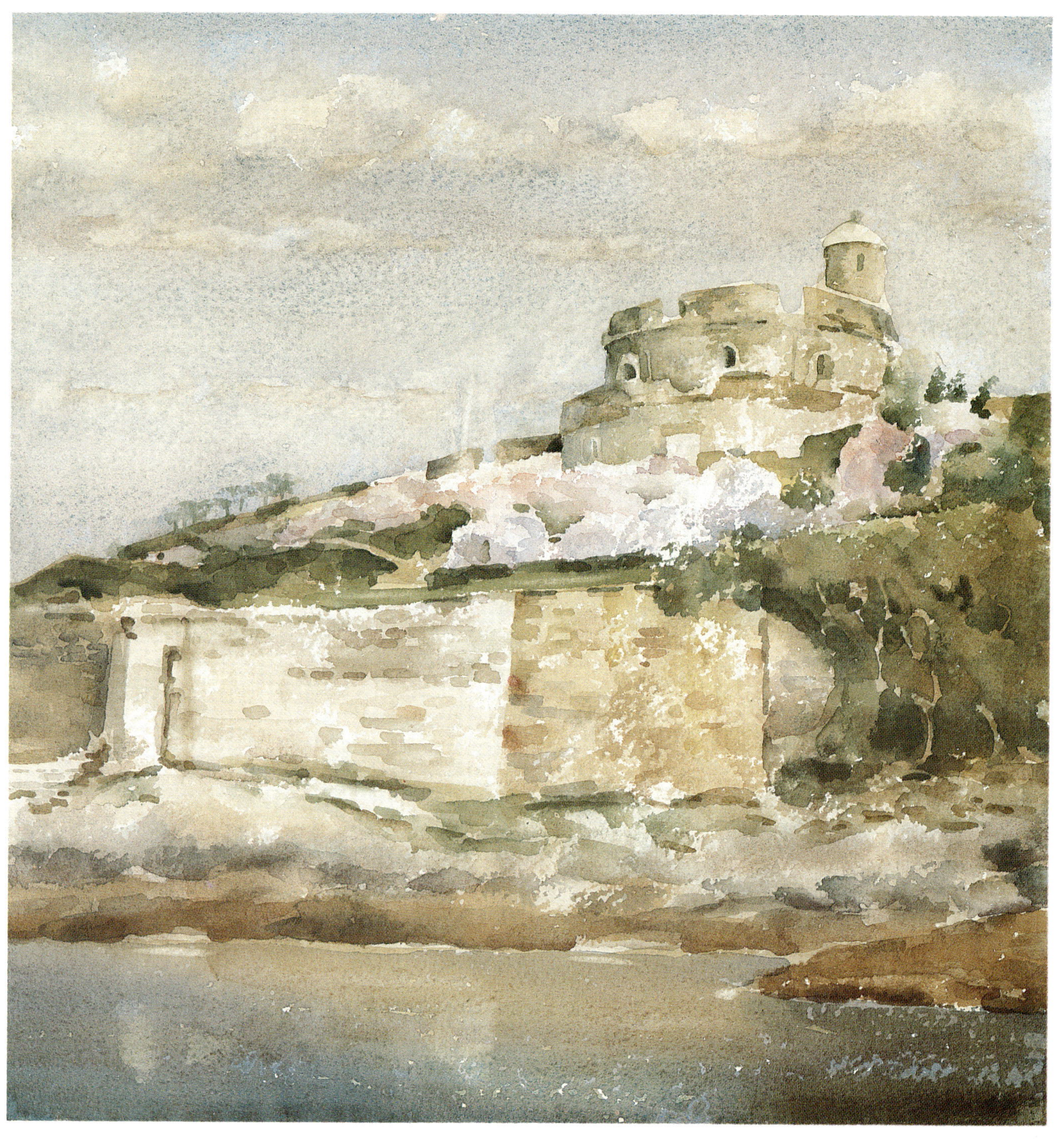

ST. MAWES CASTLE

'The cylindrical stone structure of St Mawes Castle and the surrounding fortified walls bounded a spectacular array of hydrangeas – .'

Four Saints and King Harry

The morning dawned sunny – though at 6:00 Epic was still in shadow and very wet having floated through a damp misty night. I sponged the dewy decks and draped my sleeping bag around the foredeck to catch the imminent rays – the bed-bag had acted like a wick during the night, soaking pints from the moist air. No other craft were on the move as I tacked three-quarters of a mile over calm water to Castle Point. The cylindrical stone structure of St Mawes Castle and the surrounding fortified walls bounded a spectacular array of hydrangeas – the subtle pastel shades harmonized with the sun-brightened, textured stonework. As I approached, high cloud edged in front of the sun – stealing the sparkle and rendering the subject mundane. Clouds advanced and dazzling sunshine over Pendennis and Falmouth also faded. I turned into Carrick Roads.

To counteract the outgoing tide and light wind I had to row. It was a carefree oarsman who, one hour after leaving his overnight mooring, observed Manacle Point out to sea beyond the Helford River, appear to move across the entrance to Carrick Roads and finally eliminate the sea horizon.

By 7:45, the wind was on the port beam and generated sufficient power for Epic to sail. I made the most of the rare opportunity and relaxed against the painting stool while working the tiller with my feet. Between salt stained boots I watched Pendennis Point and Falmouth recede as I continued down the east side of the channel. After two miles, I negotiated the larger sailing yachts moored in the mouth of St Just Creek and headed into the tree-lined backwater hoping to glimpse the picturesque waterside church. The rapidly receding tide forced me to retreat after a few hundred yards. During my hasty return to deeper water, as I guided Epic between emerging mud banks, I sighted the church off to my left – tucked away in a secondary creek.

Around 9:30, in a strengthening wind, under a darker grey sky, Epic rushed towards Feock – at the head of Carrick Roads, four and a half miles from the open sea. The red jib provided power enough to create a long wake as the little boat hissed through the water. The wind remained strong, but seemed less aggressive after I slackened the sheet to bear away to starboard and enter the pool at the bottom of Trelissick House garden.

The pool forms the mouth of the River Fal, which narrows immediately upstream to two hundred yards, then runs north for three and a half miles. On reaching the narrows I was taken aback to find myself heading towards the bows of a twenty two thousand ton tanker. The vastness of the mothballed ship was emphasized by the intimate surroundings. It took several minutes to pass by the towering sides of the surreal phenomena, Methane Princess, for the outgoing tide still had an hour or so to run and the wind-strength was restricted by high wooded banks.

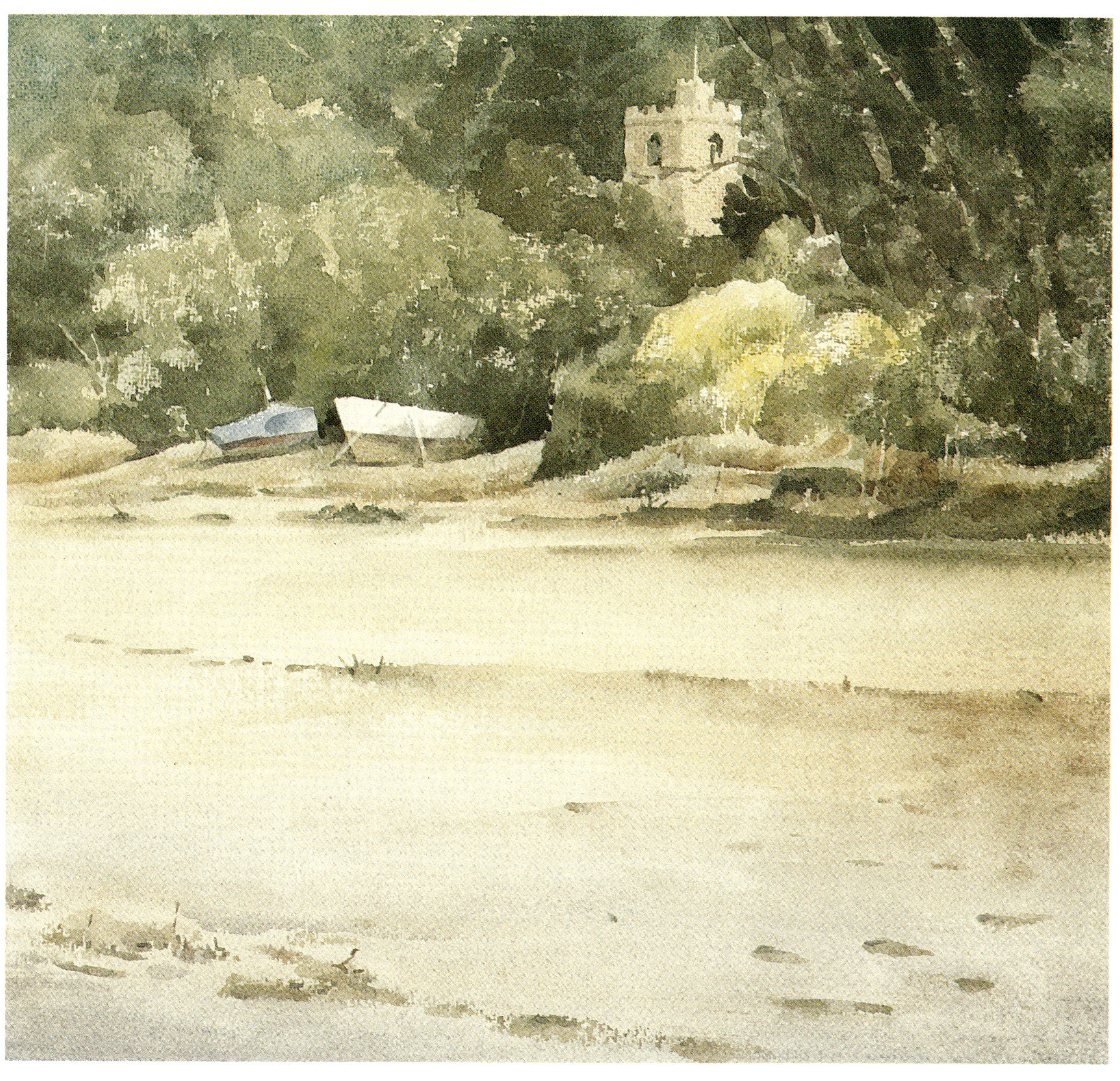

ST. JUST

'— I negotiated the larger sailing yachts moored in the mouth of St. Just Creek and headed into the tree-lined backwater hoping to glimpse the picturesque waterside church.'

A mile further on I passed the peaceful setting of the King Harry crossing. Thirty or so vehicles can be transported on the ferry that rumbles across the river with twin engines driving cogs against fixed chains. The ferry allows a peaceful journey to be made away from busy roads, and shortens the trip between St Mawes and Falmouth by fifteen miles.

Half a mile beyond the crossing, on a right hand bend, stands Smugglers Cottage. The thatched, double-roofed, multi-chimneyed restaurant can be reached at all states of the tide via a pontoon bridge, which incorporates a large fishing boat. The enchanting, creeper festooned building was, at the time, the ultimate in tranquil seclusion; although the garden was well complemented with tables and chairs that suggested extensive catering. I tied Epic to the pontoon boat, proceeded up the gangway and entered the welcoming ship-shape interior which was tastefully bedecked with interesting nautical artefacts. I confronted the bar, which looked temptingly under starters orders.

The fifteen minutes before 'the off', served to finely tune my taste buds before I was called to the bar at noon. Before dining, I wandered down to the foreshore and saw Epic looking minute alongside the fishing boat. Over the previous weeks I had become used to spending prolonged hours on board and found perfectly adequate the space available for myself and accoutrements. I remembered how cramped and unstable pre-Epic had seemed when I first stumbled aboard at Lostwithiel.

Having chosen luncheon from a long table laden with gourmet pies, hams, quiches and mouth-watering sweets, I sat down to dine overlooking the river. The tide was turning and had I not intended to explore the continuation of the Fal up to Ruan Lanihorne – three miles to the east, I could have reached Truro within three hours. With mixed feelings, of contentment and melancholy, I made my way back to Epic.

I missed the Fal junction somehow (even at low tide it is a hundred yards wide) and kept to the main channel which became the Truro River – pretty awful navigation. One and a half miles on there was another confluence. I opted to fork right, towards Tresillian – where I hoped I could leave Epic for the weekend. The final half mile before turning into the Tresillian River was accomplished with much tacking across a strong gusty wind that blew down from Malpas. I had little time to assess the merits of the village as I avoided boats moored near the junction, but I did notice a section of pontoons providing berths for a dozen or so craft.

In sheltered waters and with a beam wind I enjoyed a gentle tide-assisted sail in silence round a long left-bend. Blue patches spread in the relenting grey, and welcome sunshine further brightened my afternoon. The rising river and wooden banks were separated by mud margins. Mud also formed a large recessed plateau in front of the picturesque village of St Clement which seemed to preclude a visit. With the wind dropping and the river filling at its quickest, I used the oars to remain in the channel as I drifted on a few hundred yards to a spot where a couple of small boats were afloat, close to the water's edge – village side. They were tethered to running lines close to a rudimentary landing spit built with rocks – obviously taken from the lumpy, mud encased foreshore. I was able to land.

I stepped from Epic onto the precarious surface and made my way to the riverside path – twenty yards away. It was supported by timbers to which I tied the extended painter. I stumbled back down to the river and cunningly placed a heavy rounded rock on the line, leaving approximately twenty feet to which Epic would ride midstream as the river flooded. On my return, a sharp tug would free her, theoretically. (I had not forgotten my previous snatching débâcle on the Tamar, but thought the scheme had every chance of saving the hull from a prolonged dragging over the rocks).

Close to the river's edge at St Clement stands a varied assortment of houses – from small cottages to ample three storied dwellings. They are as different in their construction materials as in design – a pleasant mixture of stone, slate, brick and thatch was used. When the river had risen sufficiently to carry me on to its tidal limit, I returned to the riverside to find Epic swinging nonchalantly to her rock close to the other boats. I pulled the painter, reeled in Epic, stepped aboard and sailed upstream in a fading wind – some you win.

Two miles 'later', after soaking up late afternoon sunshine, I arrived at the road bridge in Tresillian; then rowed back down the river a few hundred yards to glide onto the back lawn of the Wheel Inn. Stepping ashore with no mud in sight is most satisfying; but setting foot on the green, green grass of a beer garden – well!

While testing a pint of mild (alas I had to wait several hours for a lift home), I sought and received permission from David, a most genial landlord, for Epic to remain at the bottom of his garden for a day or two. Between dining and an occasional visit to the bar I did nothing more stressful than oversee the emptying of the Tresillian River. As the waters receded the remains of two boats were revealed. I did not dwell on the cause of their sorry state – it was too peaceful an evening for such sobering thoughts. Epic would have been exceedingly unlucky to visit Davy Jones – for just over the hill lay Truro.

Finale at Phoenix Wharf

I planned to complete the voyage around high tide the following Monday morning (high spring tide), but finding time on my hands the preceding evening, and surprisingly, finding Toby and Robin at a loose end, we made haste to Tresillian. On arrival at high tide (7:30) we found the calm water had reached Epic's underside. (The tide was fifteen inches higher than on my arrival two days earlier. I had then moved the dinghy onto higher ground—with such precise judgement!).

Epic entered the water disturbing the mirror-like reflection of the tree lined bank opposite. I left the flooded paddy field-like area and set off at great pace for a rendezvous with the boys who had taken the car to Malpas. With the oar blades leaving trails of closely-spaced rings, I sped downstream. At St Clement I paused to drift quietly into the 'village pond'. The river had covered the mud plateau, forming a scene reminiscent of a popular painting. Had the pond-side been graced with an old farm cart, and a hatch-back exchanged for horses, I would have beheld a Constable. There was even a dog at the pond's edge. (A police dog perhaps).

Epic was soon tethered to one of the pontoons I had noticed during my earlier windward passage. I sought permission for an overnight berth and was informed that the proprietor could be located a few yards up the hill. I found the 'pontoon man' on the veranda outside the Heron public house sitting a few yards from my sons. After booking a berth I returned to Epic to make her secure. The water reflected the thin pearly pink clouds that veiled the evening sun and I hoped the next day would dawn as fine for my two mile trip to Truro.

In lighthearted mood we sipped our drinks while overlooking the stunning river panorama. Toby and Robin told tales of an intrepid mariner, wont to voyage up to half a mile from habitation at times, employing an innate, uncanny sonar-like sense for seeking handy hostelries.

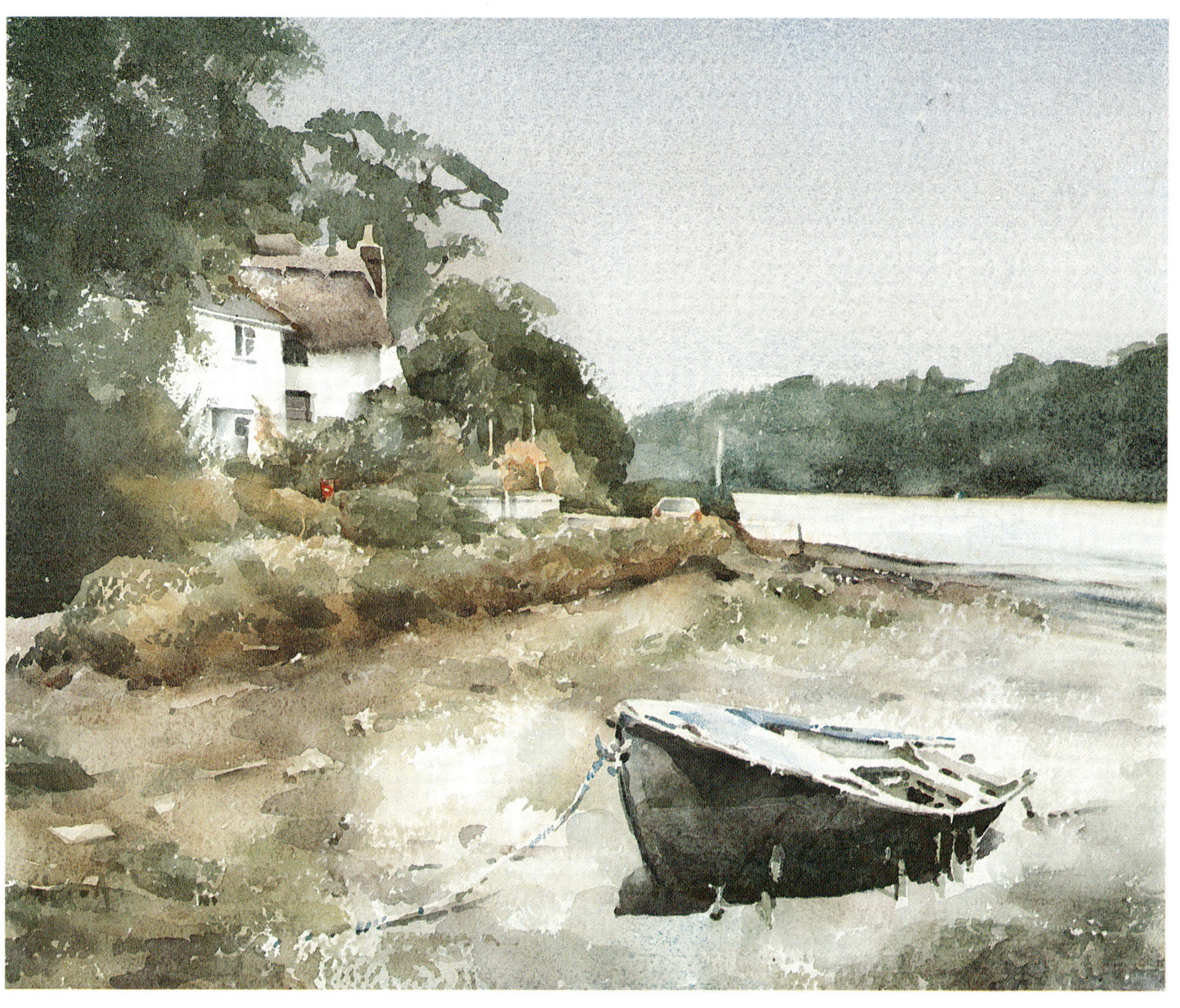

ST. CLEMENT

'Mud also formed a large recessed plateau in front of the picturesque village of St Clement which seemed to preclude a visit.'

It was much easier to set off from the pontoons at Malpas, with the rising tide to help me to Truro, than it would have been to launch down the bank and through the muddy boat graveyard at Tresillian. The Sunday evening excursion had also saved me making a three and a half mile journey against the tide at a very early hour.

The mist was clearing and peace reigned as I walked down to the boat-yard to rejoin the ready-rigged Epic at the pontoon. At 7:00 when I cast off, the village and river were deserted. The weather was almost identical to that enjoyed ten hours earlier – the difference being the position of the veiled morning sun – it was set to rise.

With slow easy strokes I rounded 'Malpas Point' and soon sighted the principle pinnacle of the Cathedral in the misty blue. It was two miles away and hardly discernible but I had been expecting to glimpse the symbolic finishing post. I felt uneasy and a little sad. The feeling was similar to the apprehension I felt when setting off from Morwellham. My trip somehow had its own time and space – separated from the real world order. The 'introduction' and 'final chapter' needed a synchronization period, and it was the returning to normality that made me feel uncomfortable.

The smaller twin spires took form as the trees to port were exchanged for wharfs, and nature's sea and tide-line tangs were replaced by industrial odours. A throbbing generator drowned the restful sound of my lightly splashing oars and was replaced, as I neared a mini residential dock-land type development, by the distant hum of motor traffic. I imposed on a sleepy row of old waterside factories. Their vast doorways led nowhere. No hanging hooks; no cargoes to be lowered to barges. The weary structures reflected their presence in forlorn contrast to the red rimmed supermarket that stood opposite and obscured for a while the triple reflections of the City Spires. (Perhaps one day the tired buildings will be rejuvenated, and the water-ways taken back into the heart of a city that was desecrated by a dual carriage-way).

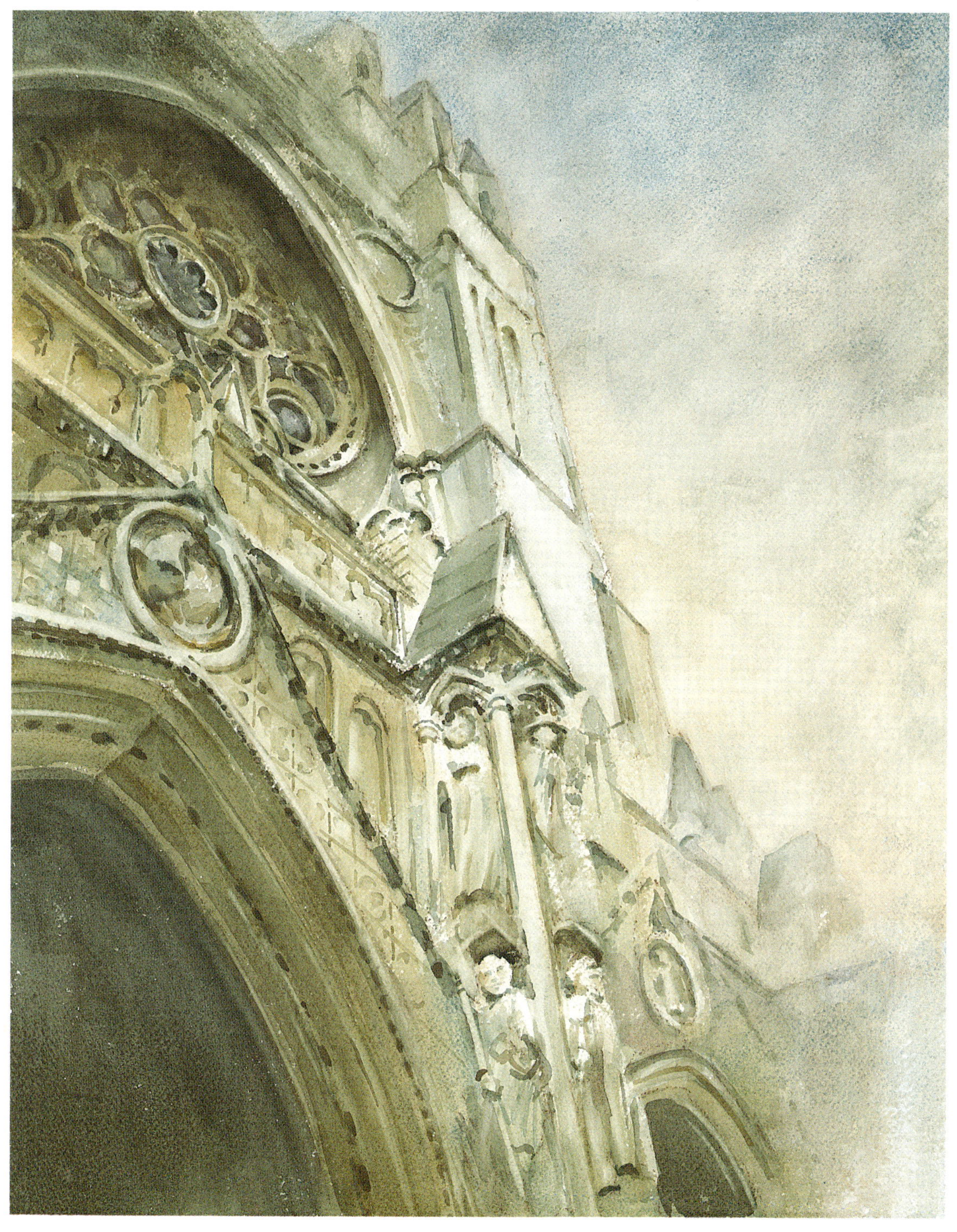

TRURO CATHEDRAL

With the mast down, the extreme height of the 'spring loaded' river still prevented Epic from passing under the road bridges. While I waited for the level to drop sufficiently, I tied alongside Phoenix Wharf—opposite the Radio Cornwall building. *(I had been interviewed prior to the launch of my previous book and as I was floating around nearby I decided to call and leave a message for the presenter, informing him of the present venture).* At radio reception I was asked to call back later—it was rather early.

A minute after rejoining Epic, I had unscrewed a shackle, laid the mast on the boat and was heading towards the first road bridge. There seemed ample headroom (about three feet) when I entered the space beneath the highway, but by the time I reached the far side the clearance had halved and I pressed my head on the gunwale as coarse concrete passed an inch from my cheek—it was a close shave. I glided into the sunshine and soon passed under a graceful, shallow-arched, timber foot-bridge, then on through the stone archway of the Bridge Street bridge. From there I beheld the Cathedral's sun drenched east side. Set against a deep blue sky, the powerful edifice with shimmering reflections completed the picture.

Assisted by the falling tide I returned to Phoenix Wharf to be re-acquainted with the radio presenter. He was due on the air within four minutes, so it was with some surprise that I received his suggestion that we perform a live interview, afloat on Epic, the following morning. Shortly afterwards I discussed the details with Rebecca as I floated (in Epic) beneath the balcony of Radio Cornwall.

'Wherefore art —' (I jest) 'Same time, same place; see you tomorrow', was the essence of the arrangements.

The following morning was misty with a promise of precipitation. Fortunately, the harbour people allowed me to moor Epic overnight against a floating pontoon one hundred yards from the radio studios. That kindness enabled me to be on station without complication. I cleared and sponged the damp decks and placed a piece of polystyrene over the mast step to create a comfortable seat for the interviewer.

In the vicinity of Phoenix Wharf, with background noises of oars on rowlocks, distant traffic and parrot-like squeaks emanating from Ted's foam seat as it moved on the wet deck, we chatted about the trip, and as we did so it began to rain!

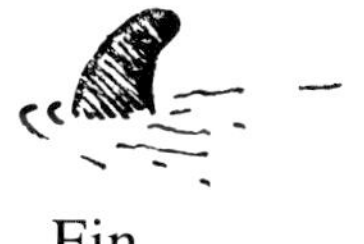

Fin.

Postamble

On the lawn, outside the window, rests the very ordinary plywood dinghy in which I planned to paint the rivers of south Cornwall. The post-trip paintings complete the pictorial record of a project modified by unfavourable weather. The elements added to the story as my mini-voyage progressed and became a challenge to reach Truro.

The Mirror did much more than transport me to painting locations – it carried me to adventure. If one can have affection for plywood, it is with more than a tinge that I look at the ordinary little dinghy that became 'Epic'.

I raise the glass, gleaned from the Tamar mud, and wish fair weather to shoe-string wanderers. Think small; cheers.

David Weston, Mevagissey.

April 1992.

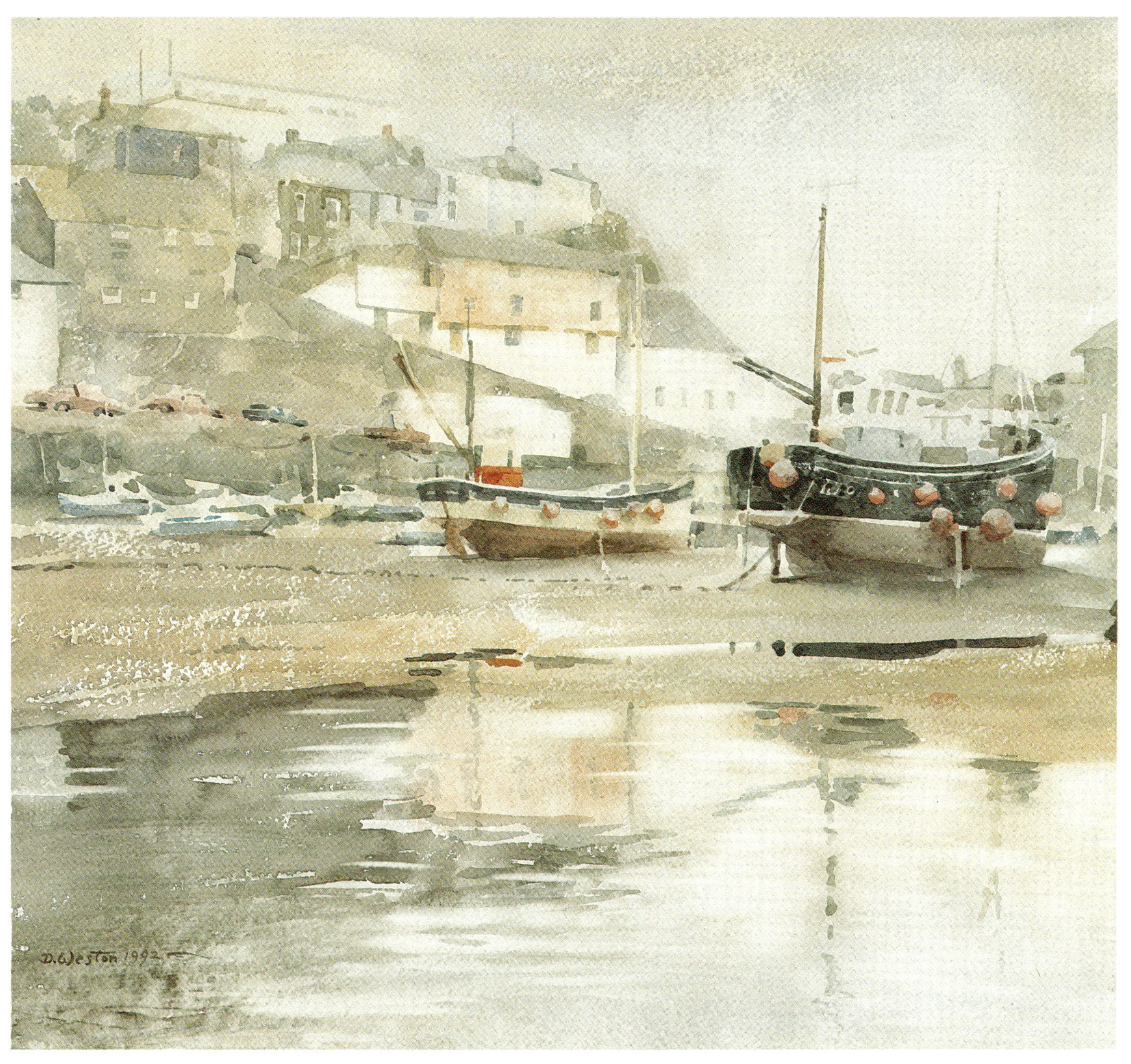

INNER HARBOUR, Mevagissey